BRIGHT NOTES

ODE TO A GRECIAN URN AND OTHER WORKS BY JOHN KEATS

Intelligent Education

Nashville, Tennessee

BRIGHT NOTES: Ode to a Grecian Urn and Other Works
www.BrightNotes.com

No part of this publication may be used or reproduced in any manner whatsoever without written permission, except in the case of brief quotations in critical articles and reviews. For permissions, contact Influence Publishers http://www.influencepublishers.com.

ISBN: 978-1-645424-66-6 (Paperback)
ISBN: 978-1-645424-67-3 (eBook)

Published in accordance with the U.S. Copyright Office Orphan Works and Mass Digitization report of the register of copyrights, June 2015.

Originally published by Monarch Press.
Elliot L. Gilbert, 1965
2020 Edition published by Influence Publishers.

Interior design by Lapiz Digital Services. Cover Design by Thinkpen Designs.

Printed in the United States of America.

Library of Congress Cataloging-in-Publication Data forthcoming.
Names: Intelligent Education
Title: BRIGHT NOTES: Ode to a Grecian Urn and Other Works
Subject: STU004000 STUDY AIDS / Book Notes

CONTENTS

1) Introduction to John Keats — 1

2) Sonnets — 8

3) Endymion — 25

4) Hyperion, and the Fall of Hyperion, A Dream — 34

5) Lamia — 44

6) Ode to Psyche — 47

7) Ode to a Nightingale — 53

8) Ode on a Grecian Urn — 59

9) Ode on Melancholy — 71

10) Ode on Indolence — 75

11)	Survey of Criticism	77
12)	Essay Questions and Answers	82
13)	Bibliography and Guide to Further Research	85

INTRODUCTION TO JOHN KEATS

EARLY LIFE AND SCHOOLING

John Keats was born in a northern suburb of London on October 31, 1795. His parents were the keepers of a prosperous livery stable called the "Swan and Hoop," and young John, the eldest of four surviving children, together with his brothers George and Tim and his sister Frances, seems to have lived a happy and uneventful life for his first seven or eight years. Then, very suddenly, disaster struck the family. Keats' father died in a riding accident, his mother quickly remarried and then left her new husband and her children, returning later only to die of tuberculosis, watched over by John. Finally, the grandmother, who after his parents' death had given the children a home, also died. Luckily the young Keats was not left entirely abandoned. At his school at Enfield, which he attended from 1803 to 1811, he made a lifelong friend of Charles Cowden Clarke, the son of the headmaster. However, Richard Abbey, the trustee and guardian of the family's small estate was an unscrupulous man who manipulated the funds in his trust, withheld money improperly from the Keats children, and immeasurably added to the burden of the young poet-to-be during his short life.

POETRY AS A VOCATION

When Keats left Enfield, at the age of sixteen, he was apprenticed to Thomas Hammond, an apothecary-surgeon, to begin his training for the medical profession. He did not lose touch with Clarke, however, who encouraged his former pupil to develop his literary interests and who introduced him to the work - Spenser's *The Faerie Queene* - which inspired Keats' first extant poem, an "Imitation of Spenser." In October, 1815, Keats went up to London as a medical student, still writing verses in his spare time, and as the months passed, debated the choice between surgery and poetry as a profession. By September, 1816, as we learn from the "Epistle to Charles Cowden Clarke," the decision had been made, and as if to put a seal on that decision, Keats wrote, in October, the first of his great poems, "On First Looking into Chapman's Homer."

By this time the young poet had already been introduced to Leigh Hunt and had become the older man's disciple, picking up certain vulgar mannerisms from Hunt that were to be hard to shake off and that would give critics the basis for their later, bitter attacks. But this was characteristic of the whole of Keats' brief career. Becoming a poet was to be for him like a voyage of discovery, of self-discovery. He would try everything he met with on the way, be momentarily influenced by every experience, and all the while would slowly come to a knowledge of himself and of his own voice.

The history of that voyage of discovery is recorded in the poems, a chronological study of which follows. That Keats reached his goal is clear from his work; that when he died of tuberculosis in 1821 he had not lived long enough to know that he had reached it, is plain from the **epitaph** he composed for himself and which marks his grave in the Protestant Cemetery in Rome:

> This Grave Contains all that was mortal of a Young English Poet who on his Death Bed, in the Bitterness of his Heart at the Malicious Power of his Enemies, Desired these Words to be engraven on his Tomb Stone "Here lies One Whose name was writ in Water."

THEMES IN KEATS' POETRY

The Transience Of Life

The chief qualities of Keats' poetry had their roots in the writer's early experiences. One of the central **themes** in the poems, for example, is the brevity, the transience, the fragility of life, and it is impossible not to associate this **theme** with a number of the events of the poet's childhood - the sudden death of his father, the disappearance and later the death of his mother, the death of his grandmother and, still later, the death of his brother Tom. Under these circumstances, it is not surprising to find Keats obsessed, in his poetry, with the subject of "beauty that must die." But if the reality of death was brutally imposed upon him by events, his response to that reality was his own. He might well have given up on life, abandoned it as too painful to contemplate as other men have. Instead, the very transience of beauty made him commit himself even more tenaciously to its pursuit and appreciation. One critic has said of Keats that he was "a man for whom the physical world exists," and Keats himself indicated that the quality in Shakespeare which he most admired was "thinginess," the sense of the object itself having been communicated. Before anything else, Keats was true to "things-as-they-are" in his poetry.

The Oxymora Of Life

Another insight which experience - especially the experience with his mother - forced on Keats was the paradoxical nature of the world. Keats had loved his mother very much, and then suddenly he found himself abandoned by her. For the rest of his life, therefore, his attitude toward women, both in his own experience and in his poetry, was ambiguous. He could not do without women, yet he could not bring himself to trust them; thus there came into being in his works such figures as Cynthia, La Belle Dame Sans Merci, Lamia - women who are at once enticing and treacherous like his mother and like Fanny Brawne, the girl he deeply loved but of whom he was frequently (and unreasonably) jealous.

But the experience with his mother did not only affect Keats' attitude toward women, it colored his whole vision of life, brought him to see life as a series of inevitable and unavoidable contradictions: joy as a function of sorrow, beauty as a function of death. Indeed, this insight into the paradox of life is a key to the understanding of all of the poet's best work, this commitment to light-and-shade-together one of his greatest strengths. The Greek word for a phrase - like "aching pleasure," for example - which unites two contradictory ideas in a single, meaningful term, is oxymoron (plural oxymora). It is Keats' profound oxymoronic vision of the world, his ability to hold two conflicting ideas in his mind at the same time and still continue to function, which gives his work its characteristic maturity, richness, and depth.

Negative Capability

Anyone who is profoundly committed to the world and to its contradictions, as Keats was, must, as a corollary, be able to resist the temptation to "do something" about those contradictions. Most people have fairly naive notions about neatness and order and are as offended by oxymora, by paradoxes in life, as a housewife is by an unmade bed. Such people are constantly developing theories or philosophies to prove that the contradictions are only apparent, that paradoxes can be explained, that oxymora are just games with words. Yet such simple-minded orderliness actually belies the complex reality of life, and to have the strength to resist this impulse to neatness is what Keats called "negative capability," the ability to **refrain** from attempting to shape the world and to allow the world to shape you.

Many people who claim to love the world really only love it when things are going well or really only love their own theory of what the world is like. Keats' genius, on the other hand, lay in the fact that he genuinely loved the world for what it was, that he truly meant it when he wrote:

Welcome joy, and welcome sorrow, Lethe's weed and Hermes' feather; Come today, and come tomorrow, I do love you both together! I love to mark sad faces in fair weather; And hear a merry laugh amid the thunder; Fair and foul I love together.

Introduction To The Odes

During the very week in which he wrote his **sonnet** "On the Sonnet," Keats embarked upon the most creative period of his life. Of this score of days Aileen Ward has written: "The last week of April and the first week or two of May [1819] seemed lifted out of time. The fine weather in mid-April had hurried the season forward; then for a few days the spring seemed to stand still." In the last week of April Keats wrote his "Ode to

Psyche," and then in the first week or two of May continued with four more odes - "On Indolence," "On a Grecian Urn," "To a Nightingale," and "On Melancholy." In these poems, Aileen Ward goes on, "Keats reached his own full ripeness as a poet at last. . . . For these few weeks he stood at a point of perfect balance, confident in his ability to meet the future, able to contemplate his past with calm, and rejoicing in the beauty of the season, the joy of an answered love, the delight of a mastered craft. . . ."

Keat's performance in this period represents one of the most astounding outbursts of creative energy in the whole history of art; to find its equal we would have to turn to Mozart's feat of composing his last three symphonies in six weeks. Keats had never written so freely and so profoundly before, and with his death now less than two years away, he would never enjoy such a rush of creativity again. These few spring weeks in his life were unique, and the source of his power ultimately beyond explanation.

Having said this, however, it is necessary to add that while the nature of Keats' genius may defy analysis, it would be wrong to think of the products of that genius - the odes themselves - as distinct from the rest of the poet's life and work. "All of Keats' life illuminates the odes," says one critic, and indeed, all of his life was preparation for these odes. "That which is creative must create itself," Keats had written, and had then gone on to make himself, very literally, the sort of poet capable of doing such work as this. Thus the odes constantly bring to mind earlier poems and prose: the lines from the "Epistle of John Hamilton Reynolds" **foreshadowing** similar verses in the "Ode on a Grecian Urn"; the technique of mingling "light and shade," whose development we have been so carefully following; even the transmutation of prose from the letters into the poetry of the odes. In a letter written to his sister in the spring of 1819, for example, Keats had spoken of the joys of "a little claret-wine cool out of a cellar a mile deep," and in the "Ode to a Nightingale" we find the famous lines:

O, for a draught of vintage! that hath been Cool'd a long age in the deep-delved earth...

In addition, the **stanza** forms of the odes, as we have already noted, evolved from Keats' desire to break out of the prison house of the sonnet without abandoning all structure and form. The ode stanzas, especially those in "To a Nightingale," "On Indolence," and "On a Grecian Urn" are thus quite obviously fashioned from the **sonnet**, being, in the case of the last two mentioned, **sonnets** lacking only four of the eight lines of the octave. Finally, there are so many striking similarities among the odes themselves -references to "Lethe" and "opiates" in the odes" On Melancholy" and "To a Nightingale," to "open casements" in the odes "On Psyche" and "To a Nightingale," to "urns" in the odes "On a Grecian Urn" and "On Indolence," very clinical references to life's pain and sorrow in the odes "On a Grecian Urn" and "To a Nightingale" - that they argue the existence of a patiently gathered body of material from which the poet was able to draw in producing his best work.

In the life of every great artist there are moments which seem miraculous, which seem to defy explanation, but which are also clearly the outgrowth of earlier work, the result of years of preparation. Keats' life is no exception to this rule, though in his case the paradox is somewhat sharpened by the fact that his whole career was compressed into a period of five years. Thus, confronting the odes, we are perhaps more astonished than we might otherwise have been at the unaccountable leap his genius took, and also more aware of how his great work is the result of his obsessive lifelong preoccupation with a few images and themes.

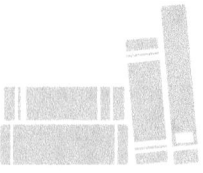

SONNETS

SONNET: "TO ONE WHO HAS BEEN LONG IN CITY PENT," INTRODUCTION

This poem was written in June, 1816. For some two years prior to its composition, Keats' had been writing verse, influenced by Spenser, among the "illustrious dead," and by Leigh Hunt, among his contemporaries. This early poetry is competent, and sometimes the appearance of a really striking passage in it, of the sort which fills the mature work, seems to prophesy the greatness to come. The **sonnet** "To One Who Has Been Long in City Pent," also titled "Written in the Fields," is representative of these first literary efforts.

In the fall of 1815, the twenty-year-old Keats had left the rural outskirts of London, where he had been apprenticed to an apothecary and surgeon named Hammond, to enter the United Hospitals of Guy's and St. Thomas' for a kind of internship. To quote one of Keats' most recent biographers, "The United Hospitals stood on the edge of the Borough of Southwark, a jumble of narrow streets, sunless alleys, and tenements swarming with the poorest of London's million inhabitants." Keats, who loved long tramps over the fields and through the woods, was distinctly unhappy in the dark city, and when the term ended in the Spring of 1816, he celebrated his release with this sonnet.

ANALYSIS

The person who has long been in city "pent" (that is, "confined") is, of course, Keats - not Keats the keen observer of nature-as-it-really-is, but rather a self-conscious Keats, a Keats too much aware of himself as a poet and determined to record what a poet might be expected to feel upon his return to the country. In particular, the boneless sentimentality which characterizes much of Leigh Hunt's verse has here plainly influenced Hunt's young protege. Keats strikes poses. He speaks of breathing "a prayer/ Full in the smile of the blue firmament." Fatigued, "he sinks into some pleasant lair/ Of wavy grass, and reads a debonair/ And gentle tale of love and languishment." (Would the poet have used "lair" and "debonair" if he hadn't needed the rhyme?) He doesn't listen to the song of the nightingale, something he was to do later with great success. Instead, he "catches the notes of Philomel," and this classical, stereo-typed reference to the nightingale has the effect of standing between the reader and the poet's real feeling, just as the word "cloudlets" seems to render the whole experience of release from the city a little contemptible.

Keats was, of course, soon to become aware of the inadequacies of this sort of sentimental poetic **diction** and of these standard poetic postures. What he most admired Shakespeare for was his ability to communicate the thing itself, the "thinginess," the actuality of an experience, and it was toward the achievement of this kind of control of language that the young poet was to move all his life. There is, however, one momentary flash of such power in this **sonnet**, power of the sort Keats was later to command almost at will. The extraordinary moment comes at the very end of the poem when, seeking a **metaphor** to describe how mournful it is that even this lovely day must die, the poet speaks of the afternoon's gliding by as

E'en like the passage of an angel's tear That falls through the clear ether silently.

The image is an extravagant one, certainly too extravagant for this superficial poem, which can hardly bear its weight. For what should have been only a conventional expression of regret at the passing of the day becomes, suddenly, an almost painful insight into the tragic human condition. The knowledge that everything beautiful must die was to haunt Keats all his life and to pervade all of his great poetry. In this **sonnet**, that knowledge is represented as a truth so poignant that even the angels weep at it. Further, the conclusion of the poem is an early statement of Keats's famous oxymoronic vision (see Introduction), his intuitive recognition that happiness and sorrow are inseparable, that men can never quite divorce from their moments of greatest joy the knowledge that those moments must end. The greatest odes in particular make this point, especially the "Ode to Melancholy," and it is also interesting to note how, in the "Ode on a Grecian Urn," the passage of the urn through "slow time," like the falling of the angel's tear through the rarefied "ether," is described as being silent. For Keats, the symbols (like the urn and the tear) of perfect beauty always exist on a plain outside of "noisy" human experience and are therefore always beyond man's grasp.

SONNET: "ON FIRST LOOKING INTO CHAPMAN'S HOMER," INTRODUCTION

Keats could read no Greek and so his knowledge of Homer was necessarily limited to the rather refined eighteenth-century translations of the **epics** by Alexander Pope. Then one night in October, 1816, Keats' teacher, Charles Cowden Clarke, introduced his friend to the finest passages in George Chapman's vigorous Elizabethan version of Homer's great works, and as Clarke later recalled the event, "Keats shouted with delight" at some of the lines. It was six o'clock in the morning before the young poet could tear himself away from the calf-bound book he and Clarke were reading, and as he walked home through the deserted streets, the lines of a **sonnet** began to form themselves in his mind. Once home, he wrote out the poem, made a copy of it, and sent it off by messenger to Clarke, who found it on his breakfast table when he came down later in the morning.

ANALYSIS

To quote Aileen Ward, "It is not hard to imagine Clarke's amazement as he read the **sonnet** over. The poem was a miracle; not simply because of its mastery of form, or because Keats was only twenty when he wrote it, or because he wrote it in the space of an hour or two after a night without sleep. Rather because nothing in his earlier poetry gave any promise of this achievement: the gap between this poem and his summer work [see "To One Whom Has Been Long in City Pent"] could be leaped only by genius . . . The unity of form and feeling that begins in the first line and swells in one crescendo of excitement to the final crashing silence was instantaneous and unimprovable."

This passage suggests one source of the sonnet's strength: its coherence, its singleness of purpose, the appropriateness of all the parts to the whole. The poem is unified by its central **metaphor**, the metaphor of voyaging for discovery. Keats begins by stating that he has traveled much in "the realms of gold;" that is, he has long been an admirer of Greek literature, which poets have always recognized to be sacred to Apollo, god of poetry and music. In his travels, the author continues, he has often heard of one particular land, ruled by "deep-browed Homer," but had never come to know it until he heard Chapman speak out "loud and bold." That is, the translation of Homer by Pope had given only a hint of the poet's greatness; it took Chapman's vigor to make the glory of the **epics** real. (Note that tastes have changed since the early nineteenth century. Today the romantic Chapman seems to convey no more of the essential Homer than does the classical Pope.) So astonished is Keats by this revelation that he must compare his metaphorical "discovery" of Homer with some actual discoveries, the discovery of a new planet, for example, or of a new sea. And so the images of seeking and finding move through the poem from the first word to the last.

But there is more to this **sonnet** than its **metaphor**. Its tone, too, contributes to its power. We have already noted the rather flabby sentimentality of "To One Who Has Been Long in City Pent." Curiously, though that poem is written in the third person, it is full of the poet's self-consciousness about himself and his feelings. "On First Looking into Chapman's Homer" is composed in the first person - the word "I" appears six times - but it seems, nevertheless, much more objective, as if its subject were as much the discovery as the discoverer. In spite of such words as "ken" (range of sight; understanding) and "demesne" (region or realm; pronounced to **rhyme** with "remain") and such a phrase as "pure serene," the work is quite simple to understand, its statement clear and direct. The richness of the poem does not depend upon the use of such words as "lair" and "debonair" and "languishment," but rather stems from the richness of the **metaphor** itself, which links the discovery by Keats of Chapman's Homer with all the great discoveries of the world, and more particularly, with the creative capabilities of men, with the inexplicable rising of men above themselves (as Keats rose above himself when he wrote this poem) in the face of great beauty. Indeed, it is significant that Keats's first great poem should be about art. In one way or another, art is the subject of all his best poems, and especially art as a **metaphor** for all human creativity and self-discovery.

One more explanation for the power of this poem lies in what Keats called, trying to account for Shakespeare's greatness, "thinginess," the ability to find the words that will infallibly convey the essence of a scene or an emotion. The last four lines of the **sonnet** in particular have this quality. First, they are remarkably specific. Imagine how much would be lost here if we were to substitute such general terms as "explorer," "ocean," and "mountain" for "Cortez," "Pacific," and "Darien." Note how the exalted calm of Cortez is set off and accentuated by the agitation of his men; the men give extra depth and reality to the picture. And note, too, how the very sounds of the words contribute to what Aileen Ward calls the "crescendo of excitement," a crescendo that climaxes in the three words "wild surmise - Silent" whose bright chiming of long "i" sounds offers such a marked contrast to the "crashing silence" that follows.

Comment

At one point, Keats was perhaps too specific for his own good, and generations of students have been able to feel superior to the poet over his confusion of Cortez with Balboa. It is not clear whether Keats deliberately made the error, preferring the sound of "Cortez" to that of "Balboa," or whether the mistake was accidental. He had read William Robertson's *History of America* containing descriptions of Balboa's discovery of the Pacific and Cortez's first view of Mexico City, which recalled a painting by Titian that his friend Joseph Severn may have pointed out to him during the summer of 1816, and perhaps the confusion was unintentional. The real point, however, is that the error is not a significant one. Poets are devoted to the communication of truth, to be sure. But the truth, the reality with which they are principally concerned, is not so much historical truth as the essential reality of their experience. Thus, to the extent that the power and the excitement and the reality of the last four lines of this **sonnet** would be interfered with by the substitution of Balboa for the better-sounding Cortez, the passage is paradoxically truer for being historically inaccurate. Picasso once said that art is a lie someone tells in order to tell the truth. "On First Looking Into Chapman's Homer" supports that definition.

SONNET: "KEEN, FITFUL GUSTS"

This poem, written in September, 1816, is another tribute to Leigh Hunt, from whose cottage Keats is walking homeward on a chilly autumn night after delighting with him in Milton's "Lycidas" and Petrarch's poems in honor of Laura. The poem says that though the weather is chilly, the author feels little of the cold and gloom, for his mind is back in the hospitable cottage from which he has just come, and he is warmed by thoughts of the poems he has been reading. But, in fact, the tone and structure of the **sonnet** are somewhat at odds with this synopsis, for the best lines are just those which describe the bleak chill of the way home, (though home itself is once more a "pleasant lair" - cf. "To One Who Has Been Long in City Pent"), while the weakest are those in which Milton and Petrarch are mentioned. In such words and phrases as "brimfull of the friendliness," "little cottage," "fair-haired Milton," "gentle Lycid," "lovely Laura," and "faithful Petrarch" Keats is indeed paying tribute to Hunt, for it is plainly Hunt's influence that is responsible for the optimistic sentimentality of the passage. All in all, the best line of the poem is the first - "Keen, fitful gusts are whispering here and there" - and it is interesting to note that Keats became so obsessed with the rhythm of this line that he repeated it in the openings of his next two sonnets. "To a Young Lady Who Sent Me a Laurel Crown" begins

Fresh morning gusts have blown away all fear and "To My Brothers" opens with the words

Small, busy flames play through the fresh laid coals.

SONNET: "ON THE GRASSHOPPER AND THE CRICKET," INTRODUCTION

During one of the evenings in 1816 that Keats was spending with Leigh Hunt, a cricket began to chirp on the hearth and Hunt proposed to his friend that they write **sonnets** on this subject in playful competition. The two poets responded to this challenge, each in his characteristic way, and a comparison of the two poems is instructive. Hunt's is entitled "To the Grasshopper and the Cricket" and reads

Green little vaulter in the sunny grass, Catching your heart up at the feel of June, Sole voice that's heard amidst the lazy noon, When even the bees lag at the summoning brass, And you, warm little housekeeper, who class With those who think the candles come too soon, Loving the fire, and with your tricksome tune Nick the glad silent moments as they pass; Oh sweet and tiny cousins, that belong, One to the fields, the other to the hearth, Both have your sunshine; both, though small, are strong At your clear hearts; and both seem given to earth To ring in thoughtful ears this natural song - Indoors and out, summer and winter, mirth.

Analysis

These lines give us an opportunity to see at first hand the sort of work that was influencing Keats at the beginning of his career. The sonnet illustrates very well Hunt's habit of reducing all experience to precious diminutives and sugary good feeling. Grasshoppers and crickets are, of course, small, but when the "little vaulter" is compared with the "little housekeeper," and then the two are referred to as "sweet and tiny cousins," we rebel at the way in which the poet forces the whole world into a single mold, and at that, a mold which seems originally to have been designed to produce chocolate Easter bunnies.

While Hunt was satisfied to describe the grasshopper and the cricket in these sentimental terms, Keats was moved to make a **metaphor** of the insects, and as might be expected, to make of them a **metaphor** for art. The first line of the **sonnet** indicates what the scope of the poem is to be.

The poetry of earth is never dead:

The grasshopper and the cricket are both singers, and as such, are legitimate symbols of the poet and his shaping imagination. The grasshopper sings all summer, and his song is of the delight and luxury of the warm season. But summer, like all good things, must pass. Winter must inevitably come, and when it does, man has only his faded memories of "beauty that must die" (see the "Ode on Melancholy") to cheer him unless he is fortunate enough also to have a cricket on his hearth, a cricket whose voice is so much like the grasshopper's that the very sound of it is able to recreate the lost beauty of the summer. The parallel with the poet and his art need not be belabored. It is the essence of man's tragic condition that all things beautiful must die, and it is the essence of the poet's business to try to rescue such beauty from total annihilation by seeking, with the abstractions of melody, and color, and words and form, to capture what is most crucial in the beautiful experience, to reproduce it, and to give the beauty a second existence outside of time, an existence no longer subject to death. The cricket, merely by calling to mind the special note of the grasshopper, brings the whole summer back with a rush in the midst of winter and is therefore a true poet.

"SLEEP AND POETRY," INTRODUCTION

One evening the conversation ran on so late at Leigh Hunt's cottage that Keats was offered a bed for the night in Hunt's study. Excited and unable to sleep, the young poet began composing some lines in his head, lines in which he summed up his understanding of the nature of poetry and speculated about his own destiny as a poet. Hunt had told his protege that he would someday rank with Shakespeare, Milton, and Wordsworth among the English poets, and so Keats confronted the question of his future with high seriousness. At this early stage in his career, however, the best answer he could find to that question was the one he set down in the "long, rambling, ecstatic" work he called "Sleep and Poetry."

Analysis

The curious title says as much about Keats' later poems as it does about this one. The phrase is what we have called an oxymoron (see Introduction), that is, two contradictory terms which together express a single, reasonable idea. Keats' poem begins by contrasting the two terms in the title. Sleep is represented specifically as unconsciousness, but beyond that, and in more general terms, it is seen as the universal and necessary yielding of the mind to the basic demands of the body and of life. It is dark, intuitive, and extraordinarily sensual even for Keats, in whose work the depiction of sensuality plays a major part. Poetry, on the other hand, is described as the highest form of consciousness, requiring - as Milton, for example, saw the problem - that the poet "shun delights and live laborious days." Keats writes:

in the bosom of a leafy world We rest in silence, like two gems upcurl'd In the recesses of a pearly shell. And can I ever bid these joys farewell? Yes, I must pass them for a nobler life...

Thus at first glance, the two terms seem irreconcilable. However, the central insight of the poem is that sleep and poetry are not opposed to one another, are not antithetical, but are, in fact, two aspects of the same creative urge, the alternation of "indolence" and "energy" which Keats had already come to see was essential to the making of poetry, and about which he was to write months later in the "Ode to a Nightingale" and the "Ode on Indolence." Perhaps the key lines in "Sleep and Poetry" are those three or four toward the end of the poem in which Keats, having indulged in an ecstatic hymn of praise to the intensity and pure consciousness of poetry, is careful to add

yet I must not forget Sleep, quiet with his poppy coronet: For what there may be worthy in these rhymes I *partly* owe to him... [italics added]

The tribute to sleep seems quite reasonable. Just as the body needs rest after exertion to prepare it for fresh labors, so the poet's mind needs to refresh itself periodically by returning to the intuitive experiences out of which all art is fashioned. Indeed, what is most significant about this poem is the way in which both sleep and poetry are defined in the same lush terms, in the same sensual images, a fact which reveals more clearly than anything else Keats' tendency to reconcile opposites rather than choose between them. If the depth and repose of the author's best work can be accounted for at all, it can be accounted for by this habit of blending "light and shade," of accepting as necessities both "indolence" and "energy."

Beyond this, "Sleep and Poetry" touches on a number of other subjects in its rambling course, among them the poet's ambition and his struggles to achieve it, his fears that he may not succeed, and his dislike of what he regarded as the pseudo-poetry of Alexander Pope and the neoclassical school. In the last lines, there are references to objects in the room of Hunt's cottage where Keats was spending this sleepless night.

"I STOOD TIP-TOE," INTRODUCTION

Written during the summer, fall, and winter of 1816, "I Stood Tip-Toe" is in many ways a poem of preparation, a personal preparation for Keats, who was in the process of becoming the poet he longed to be. It was also a preparation for many of the themes, views and attitudes which were to be more fully developed in the later works. When Keats began the poem in June, it was with no particular **theme** or subject in mind. The lines were simply allowed to run on, recording the beauties of early summer which the young poet had observed from a little hill on Hampstead Heath. Indeed, half the poem consists of this lush description, some of it rather overblown, as when drops of dew are referred to as "starry diadems/ Caught from the early sobbing of the morn," but some of it in the authentic Keatsian voice, celebrating the sensual delights of the earth. And Keats, at this stage in his development, was content with such celebration. He plainly subscribed, early in his career, to Leigh Hunt's doctrine that

they shall be accounted poet kings Who simply tell the most heart-easing things . . .

and it was to this end, to the end of pleasing his readers with depictions of nature's beauty, that he rather aimlessly heaped up the rich images that fill the first half of "I Stood Tip-Toe."

Analysis

But as time passed and the poem progressed, certain doubts about his course began to assail the poet. He felt that, as one critic has put it, "there was more to [poetry] than listing all the sights and sounds of a summer's day, however beautiful." He came to see that not nature alone but a certain something in nature - an order, a structure, a series of relationships - was to be his true subject. Instinctively he turned to the classical myths for substance in his poem, myths which had long delighted him and which he was sensitive enough to realize were not just pretty stories but profound **metaphors** for the most serious of human experiences. Famous mythological figures move in procession through "I Stood Tip-Toe": Psyche, of whom Keats would have more to say in one of his great odes; Pan, whose sorrow at the loss of Syrinx is expressed in the oxymora "sweet desolation" and "balmy pain" (the poet hinting at the reciprocal nature of pleasure and melancholy which was to become one of his major themes); and Narcissus and Echo, whose tale would seem especially meaningful to an artist.

Of this last pair Keats writes What first inspired a bard of old to sing Narcissus pining o'er the untainted spring?

a question he was to raise, in one way or another, all his life. For here, simply stated, is the central problem of the poet, and Keats' problem in particular. What is it that drives the artist? What does he see in experience that other men do not? Gradually, the mythical Endymion, who fell in love with the moon and was loved and blessed in return, came to seem especially pertinent to this whole matter of inspiration and to command all of Keats' attention in the last lines of his poem. Moonlight, which suffuses the work, symbolizes the mysterious poetic impetus, the inspiration that brings to the poet

> Shapes from the invisible world, unearthly singing From out the middle air, from flowery nests, And from the pillowy silkiness that rests Full in the speculation of the stars. Ah! surely he [the poet] had burst our mortal bars; Into some wondrous region he had gone, To search for thee, divine Endymion!

Comment

And it is the same moonlight which inspires Endymion, who stands (like Keats, of whom he is a symbol) tip-toe on Mt. Latmus' top, straining to reach the "invisible," "unearthly," wondrous region" of pure beauty. But the wedding of Endymion and the moon, symbolic of poetic achievement, is not to be consummated in this poem. Just as the crucial moment is reached, Keats breaks off. "Was there a Poet born?" he asks, and then sensing that he is not yet himself enough of a poet to answer this question as it deserves to be answered, he hurries the poem to a conclusion with the words

but now no more, My wand'ring spirit must no further soar. -

"TO AUTUMN"

This ode, though written in September of 1819, belongs, both in spirit and in quality, to the great odes of the previous spring. In one sense, the poem with its three **stanzas** of profoundly sensual but superbly controlled pictures of autumn, is, of all the works of Keats, the one in which the poet most nearly fulfills what he called his "negative capability" (see Introduction). With the exception of the first two lines of the third stanza:

Where are the songs of Spring? Ay, where are they? Think not of them, thou hast thy music too . . .

the work has no overt philosophical content; there is no sense, in other words, that the images depicted are being made to serve any ends but their own. Yet we are not, for that reason, dealing here with a mere piling up of pictures of the sort we find in the first half of "I Stood Tip-toe." Implied in the later poem, as it is not in the earlier, is the overwhelming process of the earth, the organization, the structure underlying the apparently random images of the season. Of course, Keats was a much more skillful technician in 1819 than he was in 1816, and such a line as "Thy hair soft-lifted by the winnowing wind" has enormous tactile reality (compare "And the long carpets rose along the gusty floor" in "The Eve of St. Agnes"). But what is most remarkable about the "Ode to Autumn" is the way in which, like life itself, it suggests a cosmic order while actually depicting on its surface only a series of physical events and images.

   Walter Jackson Bate makes a similar point about the "concrete exactness and fidelity" of these images. In "To Autumn," he writes, "the poet himself is completely absent; there is no 'I,' no suggestion of the discursive language that we find in the other odes: the poem is entirely concrete, and self-sufficient in and through its concreteness." But this is not to say that the poem is without wider philosophical significance. "If dramatic debate, protest and qualification are absent," Bate goes on, "it is not because any premises from which they might proceed are disregarded," but rather because they have been entirely "absorbed" in the poem and exist there wholly by implication. For example, one of the **themes** embodied most strikingly in the ode is one with which we have already become familiar through a reading of Keats' other poems - the reconciliation of opposites. Indeed, the most brilliant achievement of the poem is the way in which it manages to represent the beauty of autumn both as a part of the on-going procession of life and as a perfect and eternally unchanging moment out of time. This is skillfully accomplished by depicting autumn - which is, after all, a season, and which therefore testifies, if only by implication, to the existence of summer and winter - as participating, paradoxically, in a process which never ends. The hives, for instance, are as full as they can get, but there are "still more, later flowers for the bees" to make honey with. Reaping time has come - surely a moment of great finality and change - but though the fields are full of "stubble," Keats is somehow able to convey the impression, through his references to the personified season "sitting careless on a granary floor" or sparing "the next swath and all its twined flowers," that the reaping is still all to be done. What is communicated in "To Autumn," then, without resort to abstract philosophizing, is a profound sense of the immortality inherent in changing experience, an immortality which art is uniquely equipped to preserve. Like the Grecian craftsman, whose silent urn is unable to recreate the noisy vitality of life, Keats, in "one of the most nearly perfect poems in English," has succeeded in conveying what for him was both a religious and an aesthetic faith, a faith in the permanence of "beauty that must die."

ENDYMION

In "Endymion," written from April to November, 1817, and published as a separate volume in 1818, Keats continues a number of the quests begun in "I Stood Tip-Toe," in particular, the quest for the meaning of the myth of Endymion, and the quest for his own poetic identity. "That which is creative must create itself," Keats wrote to his publisher in October, 1818, and in "Endymion" we see the poet attempting - not always with success - to create himself, to achieve full maturity of poetic insight and expression, through the old myth of the artist and the moon.

Thomas Bulfinch, in *The Age of Fable*, has the following to say about Endymion. "Endymion was a beautiful youth who fed his flock on Mount Latmus. One calm, clear night, Diana [called Cynthia in Keats's poem], the moon, looked down and saw him sleeping. The cold heart of the virgin goddess was warmed by his surpassing beauty, and she came down to him, kissed him, and watched over him while he slept.

"Another story was that Jupiter bestowed on him the gift of perpetual youth united with perpetual sleep. Of one so gifted we can have but few adventures to record. Diana, it was said, took care that his fortunes should not suffer by his inactive life, for she made his flock increase, and guarded his sheep and lambs from the wild beasts.

"The story of Endymion has a peculiar charm from the human meaning which it so thinly veils. We see in Endymion the young poet, his fancy and his heart seeking in vain for that which can satisfy them, finding his favorite hour in the quiet moonlight, and nursing there beneath the beams of the bright and silent witness the melancholy and ardor which consume him. The story suggests aspiring and poetic love, a life spend more in dreams than in reality, and an early and welcome death."

Analysis

The fact, noted above by Bulfinch, that few adventures can be recorded for someone like Endymion, was also recognized by Keats, who nevertheless went ahead with the work, having received and accepted a challenge from Shelley to write a four-thousand-line poem within six months. (The poem of Shelley's to emerge from this friendly competition was "The Revolt of Islam.") The undertaking was a staggering one, but Keats began well.

BOOK ONE

The first book of the four in "Endymion" opens with one of his best known lines, "A thing of beauty is a joy forever," which expresses the **theme** of the poem - the perfection and immortality of love and beauty - as well as the poem's subject - Endymion's search for that perfection. Not many lines later, a group of shepherds and their girls chant the "Hymn to Pan," perhaps the most effective passage in any of the four books. It was Keats' own personal favorite, the poet frequently reciting it as a sample of his work, and both in form and content it is a precursor of the great odes, celebrating as it does the richness and fecundity of life and invoking Pan as the god of sensual beauty and the teeming earth. The ceremony of Pan over, the handsome shepherd Endymion confesses to his young sister Peona that he has fallen in love with a mysterious bright being - the goddess of the moon, though he doesn't suspect it. Three times, he says, she has come to him in his dreams: from the sky, from a well, and in a cave. Now he must search for her in these three places - the regions of earth, water, and air - and the young man having prepared himself for the journey (and Keats having gotten no further into his slender plot than this), the first book ends.

BOOK TWO

Book Two follows Endymion into the depths of the earth, where lifeless, gem-studded caverns miraculously bloom as he approaches the bower of Adonis, youthful shepherd symbol of poetry and spring. (Ironically, Adonis is the symbol which Shelley was later to choose for the dead Keats in his elegy "Adonais.") Venus is waking her lover from his winter sleep as Endymion appears, and the goddess leads the new arrival to a secluded spot where he and the still unknown love of his dreams meet briefly but ecstatically. However, when the lady departs without revealing her identity, Endymion is forlorn. He wanders on, meets two more lovers - Alpheus, the river god, and the fountain nymph, Arethusa - and prays for their happiness. Then turning, he discovers "the giant sea above his head," and knows that he has come to the end of the first part of his journey.

BOOK THREE

Book Three finds Endymion picking his way across the floor of the ocean, past sharks, dead men's bones, and long-forgotten wrecks. Here he encounters Glaucus, a terrifyingly ancient creature who has been doomed to infinite old age and who begs the young shepherd to perform a magic ceremony and free him from his cruel fate. Endymion obliges, giving Glaucus back his youth and his beloved nymph Scylla. What's more, he revives all the drowned lovers of ten centuries past, and a great celebration follows, during which Venus informs him that he will soon find his love and that he will be rewarded for his devotion with "endless heaven." Hearing this, the shepherd faints with joy, and when he returns to consciousness, he is back on earth again.

BOOK FOUR

The fourth book of the poem is complex and in many ways strange and puzzling. It begins with Endymion, fresh from his adventures under the sea, ready to undertake the third and last of his journeys -through the region of air - to win the "immortality of passion" which his dream has promised him. Just at this point, however, he meets an Indian maiden who sings a "Song of Sorrow," and though he feels pangs of guilt, he quickly abandons his quest for the moon goddess and falls deeply in love with the new, dark-haired girl. Together they rise dreaming into the night sky where Endymion awakens to find Cynthia, the goddess of the moon, leaning over him, and realizes at last that this is the lover of his dreams. But as he turns to the Indian girl, Cynthia weeps and vanishes from his sight, and in another moment the girl too disappears, her image washed away by the cold light of the moon.

Endymion now enters the "Cave of Quietude," falls into a deep sleep, and when he wakes, his spirits refreshed, finds the maiden once more beside him. Amazed at how foolish he has been, he gives up his hopeless love for Cynthia and asks the Indian girl to share a life of perfect human bliss with him in the forest. But the girl is mysteriously unable to accept such an invitation, and when the shepherd then declares that he will become a hermit, the maiden reluctantly decides to serve Diana, the goddess of chastity. But these solutions to the problem are not better than any of the earlier ones. Endymion can enjoy none of the pleasures of contemplation traditionally associated with a hermit's life, and more important, he comes to appreciate the absurdity of his notions about perfect human bliss, to see that there is more to love than "flowers, garlands, love knots and silly posies." Now he has a crucial experience. The autumn sun is setting and he finds himself suddenly touched by the melancholy of the moment. With a rush of feeling, he recognizes the need to accept his own mortality as the very foundation of love, to accept the fact that, like the day and the season, he too must die. Full of this new understanding, he hurries off to intercept the Indian maiden on her way to the temple of Diana. As he takes her hand, a miracle occurs. The dark-haired girl is transformed before his eyes into the radiant goddess of his dreams, and with Peona standing lost in amazement, the two lovers disappear together into the forest.

Comment

The meaning of "Endymion" is not always clear. Indeed, it wasn't even clear to Keats, who admitted that "the development of his tale was uncertain, lacking a clear plan from the start." The poet's own ideas about experience and art changed markedly in the eight months during which the poem was being composed, and to a certain extent, Endymion's changes of direction in the course of the story parallel Keats'. Thus, if the work is somewhat confusing, and has been subject, over the years, to a variety of conflicting interpretations, its basic movement is nevertheless quite logical and is, moreover, a movement that is to be seen often in the later poems.

Endymion, overwhelmed with the bliss of human love, recognizes that such love is necessarily fleeting and longs for something more permanent.

Now, if this earthly love has power to make Men's being mortal, immortal; to shake Ambition from their memories, and brim Their measure of content: what merest whim, Seems all this poor endeavour after fame, To one, who keeps within his stedfast aim A love immortal, an immortal too.

He set himself, therefore, the (impossible) task of loving a goddess, an immortal who dwells in a world apart from man, in "pure ether," so to speak. The ambitious shepherd must go through a series of trials, all designed to confirm the life-giving and life-restoring powers of love, but when he passes these tests and is about to claim his reward, that "endless heaven" which involves a denial of his basic human nature, human nature claims him, and on the point of winning the goddess, he falls in love with a mortal woman. Almost gratefully, he lets the goddess go:

I have clung To nothing, lov'd a nothing, nothing seen Or felt but a great dream! O I have been Presumptuous against love ...

Endymion then passes through that experience of sleep and refreshed awakening which appears in so many of Keats' poems as a symbol of spiritual growth, and having returned once more to the real world, seems ready to claim his prize, the beautiful Indian maid. But when he asks the girl to share his life of simple human pleasure in the forest, she mysteriously refuses, and the shepherd, in despair, rushes off to become a hermit. The meaning here is plain enough. Keats is requiring that Endymion try every possible response to the human condition, to the tragic fact that all things beautiful must die. The first reaction is the platonic one, to abandon mortal reality for the immortal ideal. This is what Endymion does first when he years for the moon goddess, but in the end he gives up this hopeless quest. Next, he pretends that bliss is within his "perfect seizure" in the real world, but this is just another bit of self-deception. Finally, as a hermit, he tries to prove that sensuality is of no importance, and once again he fails, the pull of his own body being too strong for him.

It is at this point that Endymion makes his great discovery. Moved to a great sense of melancholy at the sight of an autumn sunset, he is nevertheless overwhelmed by the beauty of his experience and realizes that the spectacle is beautiful precisely because it is mortal, that, in the words of the twentieth-century American poet Wallace Stevens, "Death is the mother of beauty," that the loveliness of "April green," for example, is a direct consequence of its impermanence. Armed with this knowledge and with the acceptance of his own mortality, Endymion is now for the first time able to love as only "men who must die" can love, and the stage is therefore set for the mystical conclusion of the poem, in which the "new" Endymion appears and the Indian maiden is transformed into the immortal beloved.

The meaning here is again reasonably clear, **foreshadowing** as it does the dramatic resolutions of a number of the later poems. Man, Keats seems to be saying in this **episode**, can achieve a kind of immortality, but only by surrendering himself to the "wayward and endless richness of the immediate moment," as one critic put it. Immortality can no more be an absolute goal of man's life than can happiness. Both are, as it were, achieved by accident, as by-products of the human being fulfilling his own nature. Man's job, then is to accept every experience for itself, without imposing a private meaning or form on it ("negative capability" - see Introduction). For everything has an "essential beauty," which may be defined as its innermost character and which emerges only when an individual abandons his efforts to impose his own will on experience and instead agrees to identify himself wholly with it. Endymion finds the immortality he seeks by discovering the "essential beauty" of the mortal world, a beauty which, as Keats assured us at the very beginning of his poem, is "a joy forever."

CRITICAL OPINION OF "ENDYMION"

The criticism of "Endymion" (See Bibliography - Part IV) played an important part in Keats' life. It would be exaggerating, of course, to say-with Shelley and others-that the reviews either caused or hastened the poet's death, but it is certainly true that they blighted his public literary career. Much of the bitterness of the attacks on "Endymion" in *Blackwood's Magazine* and *The Quarterly Review* was politically inspired; these magazines hated Leigh Hunt, and Keats was one of Hunt's declared proteges. Where the reviews came to grips with the poem itself, they raised two main objections. First, they were scandalized by the sensuality of the work, by what even Keats' friend Bailey called "that abominable principle of Shelley's - that Sensual Love is the principle of things." Second, they were contemptuous of some of the poorer verses in the work, maliciously displaying them and chuckling over them while deliberately ignoring the better poetry. Criticism of "Endymion" today does not go so far as to suggest that it is a great poem, but modern commentators emphasize the many beauties of the work, and discuss without prudery the philosophy it expresses, seeing it in many hints of the great poetry to come.

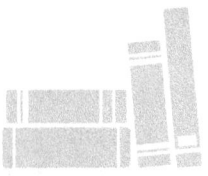

HYPERION, AND THE FALL OF HYPERION, A DREAM

Even while Keats was writing "Endy mion," in the summer and fall of 1817, he was dissatisfied with it, and was looking around for possible subjects for a new work, one in which he might avoid the pitfalls into which he had fallen in his first long poem. The subject of Hyperion came to his attention and seemed capable of supplying material for the **epic** he had in mind, particularly as it differed so markedly from "Endymion." Where "Endymion," written under the influence of Spenser and Leigh Hunt, and having as its basic symbol the moon, was the story of a young shepherd's pursuit of love and frequently softened into florid and irrelevant descriptive passages in rhymed couplets, "Hyperion" would be composed under the literary aegis of Shakespeare and Milton. It would have as its central image the sun, would tell the tale of the fall of an old god and the rise of a new, and would be written in comparatively stark and massive **blank verse**. Keats spent the rest of his life writing "Hyperion" producing two unfinished versions of it, and left the work incomplete at his death.

THE STORY

The first version of "Hyperion," written mainly in the autumn of 1818, approached the Fall of the Titans with Miltonic grandeur and objectivity. The subject itself had a special fascination for Keats: not only did it return him to the classical magnificence of Greek mythology, the vast vistas of Chapman's *Homer*, but the particular drama of the plot, dealing as it did with complex relationships between the immortal, the mortal, and - in Apollo - the artist, enabled him to explore a **theme** which later, too, in the "Ode to Psyche" (and, indirectly, in the "Ode on a Grecian Urn") would prove unusually fruitful.

The story, basically, was to begin with the deposing of the Titans - the earth's first gods, according to Greek mythology - by Jupiter, the leader of the Olympians, who were to replace them as divine rulers of the world. This story, with its dramatic transfer of cosmic power, had fascinated many poets, from the Greeks themselves (Aeschylus, in particular) to Keats' own contemporary, Shelley (who dealt with it in his greatest long work, "Prometheus Unbound"). The Titans' inexplicable shift from immortality to an almost mortal powerlessness is balanced, in the story, by the corresponding rise of the new gods from mortality to immortality. And of this rise, in Keats' version, Apollo, the god of poetry, was to become a symbol, while Hyperion, the sun god, whose place Apollo usurped, would be the tragic figure who symbolized the passing of the old order. Since Keats' interests were so concentratedly aesthetic, however, since he approached his poetry, as we have seen, with an almost religious exaltation, the emphasis in the poem had inevitably and uncontrollably shifted, by Book III, to the evolving godhood of Apollo, the artist. Thus, where Shelley's version of the Titan story, in keeping with his interests, was mystically moral and political in theme, Keats' was mystically religious and aesthetic, but so much so that, perhaps seeing his original scheme thrown somewhat out of balance by the increasingly intense personal tone of Book III, Keats abandoned the project entirely.

Of course, as W. J. Bate has pointed out, we cannot ever be really sure exactly why Keats left off writing the first "Hyperion" where he did. Perhaps, as Professor Bate seems inclined to think, exhausted by the death of his brother Tom, he simply felt his powers unequal to the job at hand. Or perhaps, as other critics have asserted (emphasizing the significance of Book III to a degree which Professor Bate believes extreme), he had, in describing the mystical process by which young Apollo became a god, as artist, accomplished what he had set out to accomplish. However, according to Woodhouse the poem "would have treated the dethronement of Hyperion, the former god of the Sun, by Apollo - and incidentally that of Oceanus by Neptune, of Saturn by Jupiter, etc., and of the war of the Giants for Saturn's re-establishment - with other events, of which we have but very dark hints in the mythological poets of Greece and Rome. In fact, the incidents would have been pure creations of the poet's brain." Or perhaps, as Bate finally suggests, the Miltonic style was both too overwhelming (engulfing the poet's individuality) and too difficult (too alien to the Romantic spirit) to handle. Thus, Bates notes, "there were the formal problems that unpredictably sprouted as he tried to combine so much. The whole attempt of 'Hyperion' was contrary to the development of romantic poetry; the romantic effort is personal, and 'Hyperion' starts with **epic** objectivity; the romantic ideal of style prizes spontaneity, and 'Hyperion' is highly wrought." At any rate, shortly after beginning Book III (which was itself apparently written a considerable time after the composition of Books I and II) Keats abandoned the first "Hyperion." But he never abandoned the idea of the **epic** project per se, and about a year later - after he had written the Odes and "Lamia" - he came back to it, this time opening with a dream vision of art, and of Moneta (a kind of Mnemosyne-figure), in which he himself, in his own person, seems almost to be taking the place of Apollo, to be having a (much expanded) mystical vision of art and of artistic divinity like that which the young Apollo experienced in Book III of the first "Hyperion." Thus the material of Book III is not included in the second "Hyperion" -"The Fall of Hyperion" - which, however, covers (indeed, quotes word for word) much of the material of Books I and II.

Analysis, Book I

The first "Hyperion" opens with a melancholy scene in which Saturn, ruler of the Titans (as Jupiter is the ruler of the Olympians) is discovered sitting "deep in the shady sadness of a vale/ Far sunken from the healthy breath of morn," and "quiet as a stone." Aged, powerless, "unsceptred," he has already been deposed by Jupiter, and his "realmless eyes" are closed in despair, while "his old right hand" is "nevertheless, listless, dead." Presently Thea, a beautiful "Goddess of the infant [ancient] world" - another of the Titans, the world's first deities, that is - comes to try and comfort him, but, despairing herself, she can only weep at his feet. It is significant that

One hand she press'd upon that aching spot Where beats the human heart, as if just there, Though an immortal, she felt cruel pain...

The process of translation from divine imperviousness to almost mortal vulnerability has begun for the Titans.

For a while the two remain "postured motionless" in defeat, like "natural sculpture in cathedral cavern." But then Saturn rouses himself to reply to Thea (who incidentally is the "spouse of gold Hyperion," the sun god whose overthrow is to be the epic's particular subject). In a kind of burst of mingled confusion and determination, the aged ruler attempts to get hold of himself.

I am gone Away from my own bosom: I have left My strong identity, my real self, Somewhere between the throne, and where I sit Here on this spot of earth.

he cries at first in confusion. Then, desperately,

Saturn must be King. Yes, there must be a golden victory; There must be Gods thrown down, and trumpets blown Of triumph calm...

But finally, feeling his weakness and impotence, he asks:

But cannot I create? Cannot I form? Cannot I fashion forth Another world, another universe, To overbear and crumble this to naught? Where is another chaos? Where?

The emphasis on creation is significant. Creation, forming, shaping, whether by god or artist -these are the essence of the divine, the immortal, as we will see again in Apollo's transfiguration in Book III and in Keats' dream dialogue with Moneta in Canto I of "The Fall of Hyperion."

Meanwhile, in other Titan realms, "big tears were shed," the poet tell us, but "one of the whole mammoth-brood still kept/ His sovereignty.... Blazing Hyperion on his orbed fire." Yet Hyperion, too, is apprehensive, suffering from ominous dreams and apparitions of disaster. Finally, enraged by the "monstrous forms" he sees, the fears and horrors which disturb his "eternal essence," he resolves to "scare that infant thunderer, rebel Jove," by bursting out into the skies before his time, but he finds himself suddenly agonized and powerless. Then he is comforted by the voice of Coelus - heaven - "from the universal space," which, though admitting that "I am but a voice;/ My life is but the life of winds and tides,/ No more than winds and tides can I avail," suggests that Hyperion be "in the van/ Of circumstance; year seize the arrow's barb/ Before the tense string murmurs" - that is, really, that he accept the inevitable with philosophical grace.

Book II

In Book II we see the deposed Titans taking counsel among themselves. The scene, as Bate tells us, was inspired by the counsel of the fallen angels in Paradise Lost, though the Titans are surely a more innocent and pathetic crew. Indeed, as their pain increases, their human quality increases, as though - as we have noted - their loss of power makes them ever more mortal. The speech of Oceanus, with its "Ulysses-like" quality (in Bate's phrase), is the most sensible and sane. Opposing the idea of useless violence, of war, Oceanus declares his faith in natural process, a faith which Keats, of course, certainly shared. "We fall by course of Nature's law, not force/ Of thunder, or of Jove," he asserts. "Thou [Saturn] art not the beginning nor the end." Then Clymene, another Titan, also expresses a kind of reconciliation, as she describes the "blissful golden melody" with which she heard earth greeting "Apollo, young Apollo," the new god of song. Finally, after another Titan, Enceladus, has once more advocated war, Hyperion himself arrives, and he is described in a burst of Miltonic brilliance:

Golden his hair of short Numidian curl, Regal his shape majestic, a vast shade In midst of his own brightness, like the bulk Of Memnon's image at the set of sun To one who travels from the dusking East.

Book III

This brief, fragmentary section abandons the council of the Titans for a description of the pleasant valley where the young god, Apollo, is coming into his powers. As he wanders, melancholy though he barely knows why, over the grass, he meets the "awful Goddess" Mnemosyne, the goddess of memory and a kind of muse-figure, who brings him to a sudden mystical understanding of his own immortal nature as he stares, transfixed, almost hypnotized, at her.

I can read A wondrous lesson in thy silent face: Knowledge enormous makes a God of me, Names, deeds, grey legends, dire events, rebellions, Majesties, sovran voices, agonies, Creations and destroyings, all at once Pour into the wide hollows of my brain And deify me ...

The last few lines, strikingly vivid and intense, make dramatic use of Keats' favorite device of the oxymoron to describe the young singer's mystical assumption of godhood.

Struggling in the grip of newly awakened divinity, he seems to Keats like "one who should take leave/ Of pale immortal death, and with a pang/ As hot as death's is chill, with fierce convulse/ Die into life ... " It is the old subject of art, of the poet who mysteriously makes himself (and in so doing achieves immortality) that Keats is concerned with here, and as we remarked before, it seems almost as though he had been distracted by its endless fascination from his original plan for the poem, or else as though, for Keats, the whole process of creation leads up to the transfigured, godlike power of the artist.

"THE FALL OF HYPERION," INTRODUCTION

As we have noted already, Keats abandoned the earlier poem's attempt at Miltonic objectivity and opened his new version with a subjective declaration of the ultimate meaning of art, of poetry, to the poet himself. This avowal of faith, as it were, is cast in the form of a dream vision, a literary device which dates back to such great medieval writers as Chaucer and Langland in England, Guillaume de Lorris in France, and, of course, Dante in Italy.

Analysis

Thus the poet finds himself - in his dream - in a mysterious forest, before a strangely empty arbor in which there "seemed refuse of a meal/ By angel tasted or our Mother Eve." Eating of the feast (in what almost seems a ritual preparation for the poetic process), he pledges "all the mortals of the world,/ And all the dead whose names are in our lips" with a glass of "transparent juice" which turns out to be a magic potion, the magic potion of poetry really, of which he declares "that full draught is parent of my theme."

Falling down in a swoon after drinking this nectarlike beverage, Keats finds himself before a mysteriously abandoned and impressive temple; far off there is "an image, huge of feature as a cloud,/ At level of whose feet an altar slept." Approaching the altar he sees a staircase and as he starts to climb the steps a voice warns: "If thou canst not ascend/ These steps, die on the marble where thou art." Struggling against strangling, suffocating cold which seems to rise from his "iced" feet, the poet just manages to gain the steps "one minute before death," and he is immediately restored by their life-giving powers. He ascends them, then, with angelic speed and when he reaches the top he discovers a "veiled Shadow," the keeper of an ancient flame. This veiled and mysterious figure is Moneta, whom we earlier identified as a kind of muse-figure, this poem's equivalent of Mnemosyne, though in fact far more powerful, vivid, and sinister in quality.

Keats' dialogue with Moneta sets forth his final attitude toward himself as a poet, as well as his final attitude toward poetry. Though fearful that he is no more than a "dreamer," "a dreaming thing,/ A fever of [him]self," he finally gains courage to identify himself with the true poets. Indeed, though he is still not quite certain of his ultimate stature, his devotion to true poetry is so intense that he calls on Apollo to destroy "all mock lyrists, large self-worshippers/ And careless Hectorers in proud bad verse ... Though I breathe death with them it will be life/ To see them sprawl before me into graves."

Finally, at his repeated request, Moneta reveals herself to him - a revelation of the fearful, unchanging spirit of art, tragic and yet eternal. Most terrifying are her eyes, which are "half closed" and seem "visionless entire ... Of all external things - they saw me not,/ But, in blank splendour, beam'd like the mild moon,/ Who comforts those she sees not, who knows not/ What eyes are upward cast." One of the greatest images in all poetry, this image serves not only to summarize Keats' ultimate vision of art, and of divine wisdom, turned in on itself in subjective splendor, but also to lead into a discussion of "what high tragedy/ In the dark secret Chambers of her skull/ Was acting, that could ... fill with such a light/ Her planetary eyes." This tragedy, of course, is none other than the Fall of Hyperion, the tragedy of the deposed Titans, the outlines of which were discussed in connection with the first "Hyperion." Thus the poet is now transported to the scene of that first work, and in a rather more complicated way (with occasional switchings back to himself and Moneta interpolated among the **episodes** of the earlier story) the whole tale is retold. We can see, easily enough, its relationship to Moneta, for it is the shrine of these giants, these deposed gods, whom Moneta guards. This huge, mysterious, empty temple is their temple, and, as always for Keats, his muse is his guide to all the majesties of religion, all the divine forgotten majesties of man's past.

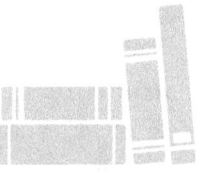

LAMIA

"Lamia," the last of Keats' narrative poems, is based on an anecdote included by Burton in his *Anatomy of Melancholy*.

"Philostratus, in his fourth book de Vita Apollonii, hath a memorable instance in this kind, which I may not omit, of one Menippus Lycius, a young man twenty-five years of age, that going between Cenchreas and Corinth, met such a phantasm (a lamia or vampire-serpent) in the habit of a fair gentlewoman, which taking him by the hand, carried him home to her house, in the suburbs of Corinth, and told him she was a Phoenician by birth, and if he would tarry with her, he would hear her sing and play, and drink such wine as never any drank, and no man should molest him; but she, being fair and lovely, would live and die with him, that was fair and lovely to behold. The young man, a philosopher, otherwise staid and discreet, able to moderate his passions, though not this of love, tarried with her a while to his great content, and at last married her, to whose wedding, amongst other guests, came Apollonius; who, by some probable conjectures, found her out to be a serpent, a lamia; and that all her furniture was, like Tantalus' gold, described by Homer, no substance but mere illusions. When she saw herself descried, she wept, and desired Apollonius to be silent, but he would not be moved, and thereupon she, plate, house, and all that was in it, vanished in an instant; many thousands took notice of his fact, for it was done in the midst of Greece."

Analysis

The appeal of this story to Keats is understandable. Lamia is the sort of woman who had always fascinated him; both enticing and treacherous, she is a more fully developed version of La Belle Dame Sans Merci. Then, the plot turns on the matter of illusion and the awakening from illusion, a subject which had always attracted the poet and which he had already treated in such poems as "The Eve of St. Agnes" and the "Ode of a Nightingale." Keats' additions to Burton's story indicate that the subject of illusion was indeed uppermost in his mind as he worked out the new poem. Specifically, the fact that in "Lamia" it is Lycius and not Lamia who tries to silence Apollonius places the young man at the center of the poem, depicts him as himself very much involved in fostering the illusion under which he labors. Moreover, this personal commitment of his is further emphasized when, at the disappearance of Lamia, he dies, his death raising questions which cannot easily be resolved and which Keats makes no effort to resolve. For example, is Lycius' death the result of taking Apollonius' advice or of ignoring it? Does the young man die because he has loved Lamia or because he has lost her?

The figure of Lycius, torn between "the perilous enchantment of Lamia and the inhuman rationalism of Apollonius," has inspired much analysis. Aileen Ward sees in this story Keats' own despair of resolving his contradictory feelings for Fanny Brawne and his friend Charles Brown; Victorian commentators treat the poem as an allegory in which cold, machinelike intellect (a la Dickens' *Hard Times*) snuffs out love and poetry;

other critics feel the tale is intended to show that corruption, however attractive its disguise, will inevitably reveal itself to the searching eye of truth.

As we have said, Keats deliberately avoided giving pat answers to the questions Raised by his poem. He did this in part out of his instinctive distrust of easy solutions, in part as a reaction against the sentimental taking-of-sides which he felt had marred "The Eve of St. Agnes, "which was written in the full flush of the poet's love for Fanny Brawne. Later that love having been somewhat darkened by circumstances, the poem began to cloy and Keats' aim in "Lamia" was apparently to achieve an aloofness in telling of the tale that would banish all sentimentality. Thus "Lamia" is written not in the lush Spenserian **stanzas** of "The Eve of St. Agnes," but in the stripped-bare **couplets** of Dryden which Keats had recently been studying and which he brilliantly adapted to his new tale.

ODE TO PSYCHE

This great secular hymn, with its long irregular **stanzas** - developed at least in part out of the **sonnet** form - was the first of Keats' famous odes to be written in the spring of 1819. The poet labored long and hard over it, or so he declared in a letter to his brother and sister-in-law, George and Georgina, with which he enclosed a draft of the poem. "The following Poem," he wrote, "-the last I have written is the first and the only one with which I have taken even moderate pains-I have for the most part dash'd of[f] my lines in a hurry-This I have done leisurely-I think it reads the more richly for it and will I hope encourage me to write other thing[s] in even a more peaceable and healthy spirit." And as W. J. Bate has pointed out, the poet's efforts were not in vain, for within a month he had rapidly (far more easily and spontaneously) produced all the remaining odes, except the ode "To Autumn." "As so often with Keats . . . the deliberate care bestowed on one poem laid a foundation and permitted the rapid writing of another."

Analysis

The "Ode to Psyche" begins with an invocation and a description which return us to the classical sylvan landscape of "Endymion" and the "Hyperion" fragment. Before copying out the new ode in his letter to George, Keats had reminded his brother: "You must recollect that Psyche was not embodied as a goddess before the time of Apuleius the Platonist who lived after the Augustan age, and consequently the Goddess was never worshipped or sacrificed to with any of the ancient fervour - and perhaps never thought of in the old religion - I am more orthodox than to let a heathen Goddess be so neglected." This, then, was to be the neglected goddess Psyche's celebration, a celebration in which both her nature (symbolic of man's mind or soul) and her story (her relationship with Cupid, or Love) take on central philosophical importance to the poet.

The legend of Cupid and Psyche (which Keats read in William Adlington's translation [1566] of *Apuleius* - chapter 22) is a dramatic one, a kind of classical version of the old story of *Beauty and the Beast*. A certain king and queen have three daughters, the youngest of whom is so extraordinary beautiful that the goddess Venus becomes jealous of the homage that is paid to her by people, even strangers, from far and wide. Resolving to punish her, she orders her son Cupid to visit the girl and make her fall in love with a foul and loathsome creature. But through a mixup the young love-god himself is wounded by his own arrow and falls in love with the beautiful princess. When she in turn begins to pine away from unknown reasons, her parents consult the oracle of Apollo, which advises that she be left alone on a mountaintop, where her husband - not a man or a god, but a monster, a terrible serpent - will claim her. Yet when this advice is followed, it is Cupid who comes to the mountaintop to claim his bride, though Psyche, of course, does not know his true identity. For a while the pair are blissfully happy, meeting only by night, in the dark. But soon Psyche's older sisters, always jealous of her beauty and popularity, begin to plague her with malicious hints and doubts. How does she know, they ask, that her hitherto unseen husband is not after all the terrible serpent

Apollo's oracle had predicted? At last, distraught, Pysche yields to temptation, and though her husband has warned her that she must never under any circumstances look upon him, she lights a torch and sees to her astonished relief that she is wed, not to a serpent, but to Love himself. The allegorical implications of her discovery are, of course, obvious. In the end, though the pair are temporarily separated by Psyche's rashness, after many sufferings and trials they are reunited in heaven, symbolizing, finally, the perfect union in man at his most blessed of mind and heart, soul and body, thought and love.

All this, of course, all the intricate paraphernalia of this legend, is simply part of the background of Keats' poem, which, as we have seen, is not a narrative but a hymn, a kind of elaborate descriptive invocation of the goddess, a song in praise of her spirit, the spirit in whose honor (and in whose manner) Keats, a latter-day disciple, plans to make his own soul.

Lines 1 - 4, as we already noted, invoke the goddess. Then in lines 5 - 23, the rest of **stanza** one, the poet describes a vision of her which he has just had. Professor Bate notes that some aspects of this description's style seem to revert to the slightly banal, sugary manner of Keats' earliest poems: "fainting with surprise," for instance, or, worse, "O happy, happy dove . . . His Psyche true!" (where "dove" obviously has no function except to **rhyme** with "love"). This occasional sentimentality is all the more surprising because Keats claimed to have worked so hard on the poem. But perhaps, as Bate suggests, the poet was so occupied with his metrical experiments - his development of a new **stanza** form for the ode -and with his intellectually charged subject matter, that he barely noticed these now unusual flaws in his work. At any rate, much of the description in **stanza** one has the sureness and concreteness, the rich and vivid detail, with which every "rift" of "The Eve of St. Agnes," his last major poem, was certainly "laden." The "hush'd, cool-rooted flowers," for instance, are carefully and sensually depicted, while the "bedded grass" in which the lovers lie reminds us of the "pleasant lair" of grass in which Keats himself so often dreamed out his poems (cf. "Sleep and Poetry," "Endymion," "I Stood Tiptoe," etc.), though the phrase may also have been suggested by Adlington's "bed of sweet and fragrant flowers." At any rate, here the old "lair" is described with a realistic vividness that may have been lacking in some of its earlier appearances.

In **stanza** two Keats turns from the concrete immediacy of his vision of the goddess and her lover in the grass to a more abstract discussion of her beauty and of the state of her religion. Since, as he reminded George, she is the "latest born" of all the Olympian hierarchy of gods, she has no established church: "No shrine, no grove, no oracle, no heat/ of pale - mouth'd prophet dreaming!" Yet, though never worshiped, Psyche-symbolic of man's soul, with all its divine potential - is far "fairer" than any of that now "faded" and obsolete canon of immortals.

In **stanza** three Keats begins to outline what will be his own relationship to Psyche. Though he lives "too late" for the "antique vows" of old religions, indeed, by his own admission, of all established churches, Keats is yet able to "see, and sing, by my own eyes inspir'd." He can, in other words, create himself as a poet, make his own soul, for there is no religion to make it for him, no "fond believing lyre" to accompany his song. The days of holiness are past, the days "when holy were the haunted forest boughs,/ Holy the air, the water, and the fire." Yet even so, self-inspired, Keats will, all by himself, constitute a religion of the goddess Psyche, a secular religion, really, a religion of man's mind.

In **stanza** four Keats elaborates this idea, which is, indeed, the central idea of the poem. Note that he will "build a fane [shrine]/ In some untrodden region of [his] mind" - the mind of which the goddess Psyche, to whom the shrine is dedicated, is, paradoxically enough, a symbol. Here "branched thoughts, new grown with pleasant pain" (thus oxymoronically including the whole range of experience that supplies the materials of both art and religion) "instead of pines shall murmur in the wind," while dark trees will climb high along the wild ridges of steep mountains (recalling the mountaintop of the original legend, perhaps). And "in the midst of this wide quietness"-all, we must remember, within his mind-the poet will "dress" a "rosy sanctuary . . ./ With the wreath'd trellis of a working brain,/ . . . With all the gardener Fancy e'er could feign,/ Who breeding flowers, will never breed the same." These lines, probably the most important in the poem, get at the essential relationship between art, religion, and man's mind which is, after all, Keats' main reason for addressing such an extravagant ode to Psyche in the first place. The poet has built a structure, like nested Chinese boxes, of mind within mind (the "working brain" producing flowers of Fancy within the "wide quietness" of the mind, all in honor of the goddess of the mind), and in this framework he is able to express what he believes true holiness to be "in these days so far retir'd/ From happy pieties." No longer the spontaneous, ignorant ("fond" in line 36 connotes foolish as well as loving) worshipers of the past, modern poets must "sing by [their] own eyes inspir'd," and they must worship not the "faded hierarchy" of traditional religion but the very soul of man that inspires and makes possible their song.

The use of internal landscape here - of the whole elaborate scene within the mind which the poet constructs in praise of the mind, as if to demonstrate his own mind's powers - is, of course, quite modern, almost symbolist in quality. Yet the allegorical "gardener Fancy" reminds us, too, that there is a long tradition behind this seemingly modern technique, a tradition which dates back, for instance, at least to Guillaume de Lorris' medieval

Roman de la Rose, in which just such a garden represented the soul of man.

The last four lines of the poem bring **stanza** four, which has already reached an intellectual **climax** in lines 59 - 63, to its emotional climax, with their newly significant return to the Cupid and Psyche relationship described in **stanza** one.

And there shall be for thee all soft delight That shadowy thought can win, A bright torch, and a casement ode at night, To let the warm Love in!

Thought, with all its powers, is still "shadowy" compared to "warm Love," Keats reminds us, and the mind and heart, shadowy soul and warm body, must be mutually interdependent. In Keats' idealized "sanctuary," in his shrine for the goddess, he will help - rather than hinder - her marriage to Cupid. "A bright torch" will let her see her bridegroom; an open window will admit him to her chamber; and the soft, the ultimate delight of the insubstantial mind will be ever-present - the warm, substantial, all-enlivening delight of Love.

ODE TO A NIGHTINGALE

No one knows for certain the order in which Keats composed his odes in the spring of 1819. One conjecture, however, is that he wrote the "Ode to a Nightingale" right after the "Ode to Psyche" and before any of the others. The poet's friend Charles Brown has left this account of the writing of the poem:

"In the spring of 1819 a nightingale had built her nest near my house. Keats felt a tranquil and continual joy in her song; and one morning he took his chair from the breakfast table to the grass plot under a plum tree, where he sat for two or three hours. When he came into the house, I perceived he had some scraps of paper in his hand, and these he was quietly thrusting behind the books. On inquiry, I found those scraps, four or five in number, contained his poetic feeling on the song of our nightingale."

If the "Ode on a Grecian Urn" is Keats' most admired and discussed poem, the "Ode to a Nightingale" is surely his most beloved. The poem is so free in its movement, so apparently untrammeled with philosophy, so lush in its **imagery**, so impassioned in its song that there is no lyric in the English language to which it need take a second place or to which the heart can more freely respond. At the same time, it is full of the speculation about life and death and art, full of the "light and shade" that characterizes all of the poet's best work and that invites a thoughtful as well as an emotional reaction.

Analysis

The nightingale, for instance, which Brown tells us gave Keats such continual joy, is represented in this poem not only in its own person but also as a symbol of poetic inspiration and fulfillment. Birds have always made ideal symbols of poets and poetry, first, because like poets they sing, and second, because like poets they fly; that is, they soar above earthbound men and seem to exist in a kind of Platonic realm of perfect and unchanging beauty. It is in response to this beauty, Keats tells us in the first stanza of the ode, that he feels numbed to the everyday, sensual world of experience and change, and one with the serene and ageless loveliness of the bird's song.

My heart aches, and a drowsy numbness pains My sense, as though of hemlock I had drunk, Or emptied some dull opiate to the drains One minute past, and Lethe-wards had sunk:

The images are nearly all of anesthesia: "drowsy numbness," "dull opiate," "hemlock," a poisonous herb whose effect is a gradual loss of feeling, "Lethe-wards," a reference to the mythical river of forgetfulness. But there are also references to an aching heart and to pained senses which suggest the sorrow of the human condition, sorrow which is sweetly augmented in such moments when the nightingale sings its song, when poetry takes a man out of himself and conducts him into the realm of pure, unchanging spirit.

In the ode, Keats longs to follow the nightingale into that realm, and thinking first of alcohol as the agent of change, invokes the spirit of wine in one of his most ardent and sensual passages.

O, for a draught of vintage! that hath been Cool'd a long age in the deep-delved earth, Tasting of Flora and the country green, Dance, and Provencal song, and sunburnt mirth! O for a beaker full of the warm south, Full of the true, the blushful Hippocrene, With beaded bubbles winking at the brim, And purple-stained mouth; That I might drink, and leave the world unseen, And with thee fade away into the forest dim:

Man has many sorrows to escape from in the world, and these Keats recounts feelingly in the third **stanza** of his poem, a number of the references apparently being drawn from firsthand experience. The mention of the youth who "grows pale, and spectre-thin, and dies," for example, might well be an **allusion** to Tom Keats, the younger brother whom the poet nursed through his long, last struggle with consumption. But the bitterest of all man's sorrows, as it emerges from the catalogue of woes in the third **stanza**, is the terrible disease of time, the fact that

. . .Beauty cannot keep her lustrous eyes, Or new Love pine at them beyond tomorrow.

It is the disease of time which the song of the nightingale particularly transcends, and the poet, yearning for the immortality of art, seeks another way to become one with the bird.

Away! away! for I will fly with thee, Not charioted by Bacchus and his pards . . .

that is, not carried away by wine (Bacchus, the god of wine, was frequently depicted in a chariot or cart drawn by leopards),

But on the viewless wings of Poesy, Though the dull brain perplexes and retards:

Here the metaphoric significance of the bird seems most clear. Like the nightingale, poesy, too, has wings, though because poesy is more insubstantial than the bird, more purely a thing of the spirit, its wings are viewless (cf. the "unheard melodies" in the "Ode on a Grecian Urn"). Yet the poet maintains the tension, the conflict between the spirit and the flesh, by immediately referring to the dull brain that "perplexes and retards," that pulls man back from the heights his fancy and intuition would help him to scale. This conflict lies at the heart of the poem. In the very next lines, for instance, a moment of pure spiritual transfiguration

Already with thee! tender is the night, And haply the Queen-Moon is on her throne, Cluster'd around by all her starry Fays [fairies] . . .

is inevitably followed by the reminder that

. . . here there is no light, Save what from heaven is with the breezes blown Through verdurous glooms and winding mossy ways.

In other words, while the spirit is roaming in regions of pure light, the body remains below in darkness, and the body has its legitimate claims. The sensual pull of the world is nothing to be despised; the world offers man summer as well as winter, health as well as sickness, and in the fifth stanza Keats makes the beauty of the physical world, the lush darkness of a summer evening, moving and seductive indeed.

I cannot see what flowers are at my feet, Nor what soft incense hangs upon the boughs But, in embalmed darkness, guess each sweet Wherewith the seasonable month endows The grass, the thicket, the fruit-tree wild; White hawthorne, and the pastoral eglantine; Fast fading violets covered up in leaves; And mid-May's eldest child, The coming musk-rose, full of dewy wine, The murmurous haunt of flies on summer eves.

Perhaps by the mention of the musk-rose's dewy wine the poet is reminded of his efforts to achieve a union with the nightingale's song, and having found both wine and poesy inadequate to help him achieve his goal, he listens in darkness to the bird and thinks how

. . . for many a time I have been half in love with easeful Death, Call'd him soft names in many a mused rhyme, To take into the air my quiet breath; Now more than ever seems it rich to die, To cease upon the midnight with no pain, While thou are pouring forth thy soul abroad In such an ecstasy!

Perhaps death is the answer; perhaps death will transport him to the realm of the nightingale. After all, death, like wine and poetry, takes a man out of himself and conducts him into the region of pure, unchanging spirit. But what sort of death does the poet mean? It is plain, from his choice of words, that he is thinking of death as a purely spiritual phenomenon. He talks of "easeful death," of ceasing "upon the midnight with no pain," and this is a far cry from the wretchedness of death described in **stanza** three. Nor does the body allow the spirit to forget this fact. Death is physical as well as spiritual, and it is terribly final; thus the death of the poet will not bring him any closer to the nightingale. The bird will sing on, says Keats, but

... I have ears in vain - To thy high requiem become a sod.

One thing is clear: poetry will never die. Though the singer and the listener may pass away, the song is immortal. The very song heard today was heard thousands of years ago; thus, though there may be no personal survival for the poet, or for man in general, there is something that survives somewhere. This is the crucial fact at the center of the eighth and final **stanza** of the ode.

That **stanza** begins with the poet bidding farewell to the nightingale. He cannot follow it as he had hoped; he had only momentarily been separated from himself by its song. Even as he listens, the melody fades into the distance like an illusion.

Adieu! the fancy cannot cheat so well As she is fam'd to do, deceiving elf. Adieu! adieu! thy plaintive anthem fades Past the near meadows, over the still stream, Up the hill-side; and now 'tis buried deep In the next valley-glades:

But the question raised by the previous **stanza** still lingers on. The poet seems to have returned to reality after his flight of fancy, but has he in fact done so? How should we define reality? What is more real, the "real" life of a "real" human being, which is nevertheless over and forgotten in a few years, or the fanciful song of the nightingale, which for all that it goes on "viewless wings," has indisputably and solidly survived for centuries? To put the question this way is to understand why the ode ends on its ambiguous and typically Keatsian note:

Was it a vision, or a waking dream? Fled is that music: - do I wake or sleep?

ODE ON A GRECIAN URN

This ode is frequently treated as Keats' central poem, as a key to the understanding and appreciation of all his work, and with its reiteration of all the major themes, its richness of **imagery**, its superb craftsmanship, it is quite capable of filling such a role. Literally hundreds of interpretations have been offered of it, no one of which, as Walter Jackson Bate has said, "satisfies anyone except the interpreter," for "too many different elements converge" in these **stanzas** to make for an easy consensus. Yet though there are as many opinions about the poem as there are critics, disagreements are often limited to minor points, or to judgments - such as the important one about where the quotation marks are to be placed in the last **stanza** - which, while they are crucial to the understanding of particular phrases or lines, do not fundamentally call into question the meaning of the poem as a whole. Thus, there is general agreement about the basic significance of the "Ode on a Grecian Urn," and it is with that significance that we will be chiefly concerned here.

Analysis

The urn of the title is a decorated vase dating from the classical age of Greece, and many scholars have attempted to discover the particular urn Keats may have had in mind when he wrote his poem. The Sosibos Vase, of which Keats had made a tracing at the home of his artist friend Haydon, the Townley Vase in the British Museum, where the poet frequently went to see the Elgin Marbles, and the Borghese Vase in the Louvre have all been suggested as prototypes, but it is also perfectly possible that Keats had no particular urn in mind for his ode. He may simply have created a composite urn out of his quite respectable knowledge of Greek art, for classical sculpture - its intensity and its quality of power caught momentarily in repose - had much impressed the poet on his first encounter with it some years before; so much so, indeed, that the experience inspired two **sonnets** about the marble bas reliefs which Lord Elgin had rescued from Turkish bombardment (stolen, said the Greeks) and which, in part through the good offices of Reynolds, had been installed in the British Museum.

The ode begins with the poet directly addressing the urn as "Thou still unravish'd bride of quietness . . ."

Perhaps a curious way to talk to an urn, but if we grant Keats his **metaphor**, we can see that, as usual, he has used it with precision. The urn, we are first told, is wedded to quietness, and at once our knowledge of the poet's earlier work suggests that in this decorated vase we have one more symbol of perfect beauty, a symbol which, like the angel's tear in "To One Who Has Been Long in City Pent," or like the star in the **sonnet** "Bright Star," exists outside of the sphere of human activity, apart from the movement and change of life, untouched by time and death. The adjective "unravish'd" helps to make this point, for while the urn has no doubt long been wedded to quietness, it is still in the condition of a bride before the consummation of her marriage, that is, untouched, perfect, uninvolved in the process of life. The word "unravished" also invites the reader to make a value judgment. For, while perfection and spotlessness are good things, is not the thought of a "still unravish'd bride" a little sad, perhaps even repugnant? Might not withdrawal from life be too high a price to pay for perfection? These questions, raised, by implication, in the very first line of the poem, are to be the central issues of the ode.

In the second line we learn still more about the urn's life and background; it is, we are told, a

... foster-child of silence and slow time..."

Again Keats is precise. The urn is a foster-child; then who were its original parents? It is reasonable to suppose that the maker of the urn and the world in which the maker lived - antique Greece -were the urn's parents, and that with their passing, the work of art became the ward, so to speak, of silence and slowly passing time. The phrase "Now he belongs to the ages" comes to mind here. Notice the exactness of the words "slow time." The urn, being matter, is in the long run no more immortal than man. But while time does not stand still for it, it moves very slowly, and so far as any particular generation of men is concerned, the vase is a fitting symbol of unchanging perfection and beauty.

In the next two lines of the ode, Keats defines the urn's role more clearly, speaking of the artifact as a

Sylvan historian, who canst thus express A flowery tale more sweetly than our **rhyme** ...

The urn, then, is an historian of the rural life of ancient Greece, and as such performs the task of rescuing life and beauty from the destructiveness of time, of freezing a lovely moment and keeping it forever fresh and new. The comparison of the urn to the poem in which it is being described further emphasizes the fact that for Keats, the vase, like the nightingale, is a symbol of art, and especially of the power of art to confer immortality upon transient and fragile experience.

Finally, the first **stanza** ends with the poet questioning the urn about the story it has to tell, about the world that it has managed to transmit across the centuries to us.

What leaf-fring'd legend haunts about thy shape Of deities or mortals, or of both, In Tempe or the dales of Arcady? What men or gods are these? What maidens loth? What mad pursuit? What struggle to escape? What pipes and timbrels? What wild ecstasy?

Keats here alludes to scenes and figures on the urn which he will later examine in greater detail. The pictures are not, it appears, altogether self-explanatory; are the figures gods or men, or perhaps both? In which of the traditional Greek settings do the events take place? The answers to these questions are not immediately clear, and it seems that the viewer of the urn will be obliged to contribute something of his own to this encounter if the full "history" is to emerge. One thing is quite clear, however. The scenes on the urn are obviously full of sound and motion. Phrases like "pipes and timbrels [small hand drums]," "wild ecstasy," "struggle to escape," "mad pursuit," and so on suggest violent activity, and the very form of the lines - many short, choppy sentences - contributes to the sense of headlong movement.

Even as Keats wrote these words, he must have been aware of the paradox involved in this silent urn being so full of noise and action. Thus as the second **stanza** begins, the noise suddenly stops and the poet speculates about the curious contradiction.

Heard melodies are sweet, but those unheard Are sweeter; therefore, ye soft pipes, play on; Not to the sensual ear, but, more endear'd, Pipe to the spirit ditties of no tone:

The passage, building up to the oxymoron "ditties of no tone." is a curious one, and has even struck some readers as being perverse, an irresponsible toying with paradoxes; what, after all, can Keats possibly mean when he says that "unheard melodies are sweeter" than heard ones? Yet as usual, the poet is very precise in these lines, and his meaning in them is crucial to the rest of the ode. First, they are a statement of the Platonic idea that the things of the so-called "real" world, the world of sensual experience, are, however beautiful they may seem, only corruptions, feeble limitations of certain ideal forms which exist in serene and unchanging perfection apart from man's world of birth, growth, decay, and death. Unheard melodies, then, containing as they do the infinite possibilities of melody, must be sweeter than any number of particular heard melodies, which, after all, are merely transient, physical phenomena. The relevance of all this to the poem is clear. The urn, like the unheard melodies, is represented to us as a type of Platonic pure form, existing outside of the constantly flowing stream of time, communicating extravagant sound and motion while itself remaining silent and still. Moreover, Keats seems willing, at this stage in his poem, to take sides in the conflict he has established between the silent, unchanging urn and noisy, ongoing life, between unheard and heard melodies. At the beginning of **stanza** two, at any rate, he seems to prefer unheard melodies, which he designates as "sweeter."

Another meaning of the lines about heard and unheard melodies is less philosophical and more practical. Indeed, seen from this practical point of view, the lines express a simple and very real truth about the nature of music which anyone who has ever heard a song sung or a tune played can understand and accept. Music is an art form which makes its effect in the dimension of time. A painting or a piece of sculpture also exists in time, of course; that is, it comes into existence at some particular moment and then continues to exist, sometimes for quite long periods, as witness the urn. But it communicates, as a work of art, principally in spatial dimensions, two or three, depending on the piece. Music, on the other hand, which also has a spatial existence as notes on a page, communicates chiefly in the dimension of time, there being a time when a performance has not yet begun, a time when it is going on, and a time when it is over. Once we understand this, we can accept Keats' aphorism as the simple statement it is. For so long as a piece of music is in the process of being played, of being "heard," it is necessarily incomplete and imperfect. Indeed, no piece of music can be comprehended as a whole, in its totality, until after it is over, until it is no longer being heard. The music lover, therefore, is always in one of two conditions. Either he is enjoying the sensual delights of music that is actually sounding, at the expense of his comprehension of the work as a whole; or else he is contemplating the finished, perfect work, at the expense of the actual sounds of music. One thing is clear; he cannot have both pleasures at the same time, as Keats is at pains to point out in the rest of the second stanza.

Fair youth, beneath the trees, thou canst not leave Thy song, nor ever can those trees be bare; Bold Lover, never, never canst thou kiss, Though winning near the goal - yet, do not grieve; She cannot fade, though thou hast not thy bliss, Forever wilt thou love, and she be fair!

Keats is here describing two of the figures on the urn, a pair of young lovers beneath some leafy trees, and the ambiguity of his feelings about their situation is inescapable. It is true that a line like "Forever wilt thou love, and she be fair!" seems to support the poet's earlier contention that "unheard melodies are sweeter"; that is, that silent, perfect, unchanging beauty is to be preferred to living beauty in a constant state of flux. But what of such phrases as "never, never canst thou kiss," and "do not grieve," and "thou hast not thy bliss"? In these lines there overtly enters the poem for the first time the idea that loss of living beauty is a painful thing and that the choice of the urn's immortality inevitably involves the sacrifice of living beauty, that the pleasures of perpetual expectation are bought at the price of perpetual inactivity.

The third **stanza** of the poem continues the development of this contrast between immortality and experience:

Ah, happy, happy boughs! that cannot shed Your leaves, nor ever bid the Spring adieu; And, happy melodist, unwearied, Forever piping songs forever new; More happy love, more happy, happy love! Forever warm and still to be enjoy'd, Forever panting and forever young; All breathing human passion far above, That leaves a heart high-sorrowful and cloy'd, A burning forehead, and a parching tongue.

The last lines of the **stanza** are reminiscent of a similar passage from the "Ode to a Nightingale":

Here, where men sit and hear each other groan; Where palsy shakes a few, sad, last gray hairs, Where youth grows pale, and spectre-thin, and dies; Where but to think is to be full of sorrow And leaden-eyed despairs, Where beauty cannot keep her lustrous eyes, Or new love pine at them beyond tomorrow.

In both poems, Keats chooses to emphasize the tragic nature of the human condition - that in the world of experience and change all beautiful things must fade and die. Yet what does the poet really mean us to think of the alternative offered by the urn? What, for example, are we to make of the curious repetitions of the word "happy" in the third **stanza**? "Happy, happy boughs," "happy melodist," "more happy love, more happy, happy love"-is there not something rather strained about these passages, as if Keats were protesting too much, trying to talk himself into something? And what of the concept that opens the **stanza**, the concept of trees that cannot shed their leaves "nor ever bid the Spring adieu?" At first, the idea may seem appealing. Winter brings death to the beauties of spring, after all, and so are not the lovers on the urn well rid of winter? Yet a moment's thought raises another question. What accounts for the keen, sensual delight of spring if not the fact that it follows winter and comes as an almost unhoped for reprieve from winter's grim sentence of death? But if the beauty of spring is specifically a result of winter, what is the use of perpetual spring, what even is the meaning of such a term to men who live in the world of process and change? Keats raises all these questions and more in the third **stanza** of his "Ode on a Grecian Urn," and his answer, given obliquely in the first line of the fourth **stanza**, contradicts his superficial earlier assumption about unheard melodies being sweeter than heard one.

Stanza four begins:

Who are these coming to the sacrifice? To what green altar, O mysterious priest, Lead'st thou that heifer lowing at the skies, And all her silken flanks with garlands drest?

The passage describes another of the scenes depicted on the urn, this one a religious ceremony of some sort which is to involve the sacrifice of a heifer. The word "sacrifice," however, seems to have another meaning in the context of the poem, a meaning already hinted at in the third **stanza**, For the perfect and immortal beauty which the figures on the urn enjoy has been achieved at the sacrifice of sensual experience; the pleasure of the lovers, always just about to kiss, is offset by their inability to complete the act.

All of the sacrifices of experience represented in the poem are summed up at the end of the fourth **stanza** in the melancholy description of the little town from which the priest and his followers are presumed to have come for the religious rites.

What little town by river or sea shore, Or mountain-built with peaceful citadel, Is emptied of this folk, this pious morn? And little town, thy streets for evermore Will silent be; and not a soul to tell Why thou are desolate, can e'er return.

The picture is a poignant one, suggesting the chief drawback of changelessness. For if the lovers are to be forever happy, then the town is to be forever unhappy. "Desolate" is the word Keats uses, a powerful word that brings to an end the easy celebrations of immortality in the ode.

But the town has another function to perform in this poem, a function that is made clear when we ask the question, "Where on the urn does the town appear?" The answer is, of course, that it doesn't appear on the urn at all. Keats is merely speculating about it, inferring its existence from the existence of the people going to the sacrifice. But this is very curious. The urn, as sylvan historian, has somehow succeeded in conferring immortality on a whole town without actually depicting it. Where, then, does the town exist? It is all very well to say that it exists in the imagination of the poet, but the poet would certainly not have imagined it had he not been looking at the urn. Thus, the town exists as a result of the reciprocal relationship between the urn and the poet, between the art object and the beholder of it. The silent, timeless urn sits on its shelf waiting for a living, time-bound human being to stand before it, and at that precise moment there springs into existence, as it were at a point midway between the two, the vital, noisy life (see stanza one) which the maker of the work of art had sought to capture and immortalize in his artifact. Once again Keats, in the "Ode on a Grecian Urn," as in so many of his other poems, undertakes to reconcile opposites - light and shade - rather than to choose between them. Art has something man does not have and which he desperately desires - permanence. Man has something art does not have and which it must have to function - life. In a kind of symbolic relationship, the two fulfill one another, and so both are to be celebrated.

A number of these ideas appear in the last **stanza** of the ode, which begins:

O Attic shape! Fair attitude! with brede [decoration] Of marble men and maidens overwrought, With forest branches and the trodden weed; Thou, silent form, dost tease us out of thought As doth eternity: Cold Pastoral!

In these lines, Keats continues to address the urn, now no longer as a living thing, however, but as an object, a shape. The men and maidens are now quite frankly marble, the whole pastoral scene is cold. Immortality, like eternity, cannot really be grasped by the human mind, for which it has no real meaning, and can only be significant in a context other than its own. Of what use is the urn, then?

When old age shall this generation waste, Thou shalt remain, in midst of other woe Than ours, a friend to man, to whom thou say'st, "Beauty is truth, truth beauty - that is all Ye know on earth, and all ye need to know."

It is no function of the urn to replace life; this is never the intention of art. Its job is rather to fill a need which life creates but cannot itself supply, the need to preserve "beauty that must die," to stop time forever at a perfect moment. Thus the urn, passing down the long line of the generations, will continue to please new men with other men's joy in the midst of woes that other men could not even foresee. But the relationship will have to be a reciprocal one. New generations will have to bring something to the work of art in order to get something in return, as the phrase "Beauty is truth, truth beauty" suggests.

This phrase has always been one of the most controversial in all of Keats' poetry. It is unusual in that it is strikingly abstract, the sort of glittering generality that Keats normally avoids, and some critics have felt that the line is a blemish on an otherwise fine poem. T. S. Eliot, for example, has called the final lines of the ode "grammatically meaningless," and Sir Arthur Quiller - Couch has spoken of them as "a vague observation - to anyone whom life has taught to face facts . . . actually an uneducated conclusion, albeit most pardonable in one so young and ardent." The difficulty of interpretation has been augmented by the fact that no one knows for sure whether the closing of the quotation marks should come after the second word "beauty" or after the word "know" at the very end of the poem. The marks come after "beauty" in the 1820 edition, but no manuscript copies of the ode have the marks there; thus it is impossible to say for sure whether it is the urn or the poet who speaks the last line and a half of the poem.

Without getting too deeply involved in the grammatical controversy or in the many subtle explications of the lines which depend on one or the other reading, we can at least make one or two points about the final phrase of the ode that should seem reasonable to nearly everyone. For though the words "beauty" and "truth" are indeed terms so broad as to be almost meaningless, as some critics here contended, within the context of the poem they seem to have at least one fairly clear meaning. If we review the ode in our minds with the aim of discovering in it a dichotomy, a contrast, the two parts of which may be represented by the words "beauty" and "truth," one such contrast immediately suggests itself, that between perfect, changeless art (for which "beauty" is an appropriate term), and changing, time-bound life (adequately conveyed by the word "truth"). The expression "Beauty is truth, truth beauty" summarizes, then, the whole intellectual content of the poem, states briefly, in an aphorism, the reciprocal nature of life and art, and more particularly their identity. "Beauty is truth." Art very simply has no existence apart from life; life, in turn, has no meaning - and therefore no reality - without art, the preserver. And therefore, in a very literal sense, this statement of the reciprocal nature of life and art is all men know on earth and all they need to know (we are assuming here that it is the urn that speaks the last line and a half). In spite of Quiller-Couch's criticism, Keats is facing facts, for what other facts are there in the world besides experience and the attempt to preserve it?

ODE ON MELANCHOLY

....

The "Ode on Melancholy" was originally to have begun with the following **stanza**, later canceled by the poet:

Though you should build a bark of dead men's bones, And rear a phantom gibbet for a mast, Stitch creeds together for a sail, with groans To fill it out, blood-stained and aghast; Although your rudder be a dragon's tail Long sever'd, yet still hard with agony, Your cordage large uprootings from the skull Of bald Medusa, certes you would fail To find the Melancholy - whether she Dreameth in any isle of Lethe dull.

There are several explanations for Keats' decision to abandon the stanza. First, his poem was to be a consideration of the true nature of melancholy, and to devote the first two of the ode's four **stanzas** to what melancholy, was not must have struck him as excessive. Then, the gruesome humor of the passage may not have seemed consistent with the more serious later stanzas.

Analysis

Whatever the reasons for the revision, the poem now begins with a peremptory warning, its **imagery** familiar from the Nightingale Ode:

No, no, go not to Lethe, neither twist Wolf's-bane, tight-rooted, for its poisonous wine...

and the rest of the **stanza** continues in this vein, warning of how not to come to an understanding of melancholy, heaping up conventional images of gloomy despair for the sole purpose of dismissing them. (Keats had been reading Burton's *Anatomy of Melancholy* at this time.) What the poet has against such a conventional approach to the subject, he makes clear at the end of the first **stanza**, when he writes

For shade to shade will come too drowsily, And drown the wakeful anguish of the soul;

That is, the traditional images of melancholy are all associated with darkness and the desire for forgetfulness, while - says Keats - melancholy, being one of the most important realities of life, should be confronted with full awareness, with full consciousness of the experience.

Besides, owls, poisons, dark trees have nothing really to do with the innermost nature of melancholy; they are merely the theatrical trappings of unhappiness. The profoundest source of melancholy, as Keats saw it, is man's knowledge of the transience of life and beauty; consequently, at moments of deepest melancholy, the sufferer should make it his business to confront the most fragile symbols of beauty he can find.

But when the melancholy fit shall fall Sudden from heaven... Then glut thy sorrow on a morning rose, Or on the rainbow of the salt sand-wave, Or on the wealth of globed peonies...

This device of responding to melancholy by feeding it raises a question. Is the poet being perverse or even masochistic in his recommendation of this technique? The answer, of course, is no. He has simply come to realize, as he states very clearly in the "Ode on a Grecian Urn," that joy is a function of sorrow, that beauty moves up precisely because it is transient, and that therefore the fullest appreciation of joy and beauty demands an equally profound acceptance of sorrow and death. No one who hides from the latter can experience the former.

The third **stanza** of the ode begins by invoking this "beauty that must die" with the poignant images of "Joy, whose hand is ever at his lips/ Bidding adieu" (who has ever experienced real joy or beauty without recognizing, sorrowfully, at the very moment of greatest pleasure, that the perfect moment must pass?) and "aching pleasure nigh, turning to poison while the bee-mouth sips"; that is, painful pleasure (note the oxymoron), beginning to cloy even at the instant it most pleases.

It is not surprising, then, that "Veil'd Melancholy" should have her shrine "in the very Temple of Delight," or that she can be seen there by

... none save him whose strenuous tongue Can burst Joy's grape against his palate fine.

The image is a particularly sensual one, even for Keats, and expresses, better than anything else in the poem, the paradoxical nature of melancholy. For the man who would experience joy to the full must have the heroic temperament to accept an equally intense sorrow. This is the central **theme** of the "Ode on Melancholy," and explains why the predominating tone of the piece is triumphant rather than gloomy.

ODE ON INDOLENCE

The "Ode on Indolence" does not achieve the stature of the other odes, perhaps because in it Keats prefers to strike an unconvincing pose rather than to take a position which he cares deeply about defending. The poem is in the first person and harks back to a letter the poet had written to his brother George on March 19, describing his indolent state as one in which he was relaxed "to such a happy degree that pleasure has no show of enticement and pain no unbearable frown. Neither Poetry, nor Ambition, nor Love have any alertness of countenance as they pass by me: they seem rather like three figures on a Greek vase - A Man and two women - whom no one but myself could distinguish in their disguisement."

The poem develops this same **imagery** of the urn and the three allegorical figures of Love, Ambition, and Poesy, figures who pass by the poet three times, the third time raising their faces to him so that he can recognize them. But he is feeling so content in his indolence that he dismisses all three, Love quite easily, Ambition with not much more difficulty, and Poesy with a simple "no." The whole performance, however, is without conviction.

Perhaps most striking about the "Ode on Indolence" is the way in which it echoes the other odes: phrases from the Nightingale Ode, the open casement from the odes "to a Nightingale" and "to Psyche," the Greek vase - all put in an appearance. Poets are obsessive people who deal over and over again with the same few images, arranging them constantly into different patterns until they find a pattern that works. The "Ode on Indolence" is not such a pattern.

SURVEY OF CRITICISM

EARLY REACTIONS

Keats' difficulty with critics during his own lifetime has received great attention largely because the poet died young. There is tremendous sentimental appeal, of course, in the story of a young genius killed by the malevolence of ignorant critics, and when such a story is circulated by another poet of the stature of Shelley it becomes virtually irresistible. (Shelley, both in a letter to the editor of *The Quarterly Review* and in "Adonais," his **elegy** for Keats, indicates that he believed his friend's death to have been the direct result of the unfavorable reviews of his work.) But Keats, we now know, was not - to use Byron's phrase - "snuffed out by an article." He was much too tough-minded for that. To be sure, many of the reviews of his books were very harsh, and Keats felt keenly the apparent dashing of his literary hopes, but his experience with the critics must be seen in the light of the fact that his whole career covered little more than four or five years and that in the last of these years he was beginning to receive quite considerable praise from influential critics, both for his "Endymion" and for his poems of 1820. In short, had Keats lived to any reasonable age, and had he continued to produce poetry on the level of his best work, he would no doubt have been able to look back on his early twenties as a few not terribly disastrous years of struggle and failure, the lot of young artists everywhere.

LEIGH HUNT

Indeed, in certain ways Keats was more fortunate than most young artists. He had hardly begun to dream of a poetic career, for instance, when in 1815 he was introduced to Leigh Hunt, a liberal force in politics and an influential poet and editor. Hunt almost immediately accepted Keats as his protege and published some of the young man's poems in *The Examiner*. True, Keats would later suffer for his association with Hunt, finding his poetry attacked on the quite irrelevant grounds of Hunt's politics, but there is also no doubt that the attention and praise he got from the older man at the very earliest stage of his artistic development was of great importance to him; it was, in fact, the sort of lucky break that most young poets never get.

"ENDYMION"

In 1817, Keats brought out his first volume of poems, and the very next year he published "Endymion." It was chiefly upon "Endymion" that the critics heaped their now-famous scorn and abuse: Lockhart or Wilson in "The Cockney School of Poetry - No. IV," published in *Blackwood's Magazine* for August, 1818, one of a series of violent assaults on poets in Hunt's set, and Croker in "Endymion: A Poetic Romance by John Keats,": published in *The Quarterly Review* for April, 1818. These brutal attacks, attacks less on Keats' poetry than on his personal and political associations (Croker even confessed in his review that he had not read beyond the first book of "Endymion"), were soon followed by some spirited defenses of the young poet and his work. John Hamilton Reynolds, for example, published one in October, 1818, as did a Mr. John Scott, in a letter to *The Morning Chronicle*, printed October 3, 1818. Where the attackers had singled out the worst portions of "Endymion" to support their contempt for the poet and his friends, the defenders emphasized the many beauties of the work, and the latter approach gained an influential supporter when the famous critic Jeffrey published his belated "Review of Endymion and Lamia, etc." in *The Edinburgh Review* for August, 1820. This turn of the tide came too late, of course, for Keats to benefit personally from it; he had just a few months left to live. But it shows the growing respect for the poet's work, a respect emerging only a little more than six years after Keats had written his first lines of verse.

ECLIPSE

Keats' death was followed by obscurity. Most readers seemed willing to take the poet at his own word that he had left "no immortal work" and that he should be forgotten. The bitter **epitaph** on his grave in Rome (see Introduction) suggests that he himself expected nothing but oblivion, and even his most sympathetic readers and reviewers seemed to agree that the Lamia volume, containing "The Eve of St. Agnes" and the Odes, was full of poetic promise rather than achievement. As Aileen Ward has written, "Long after 1820 most readers remained puzzled or offended by Keats' innovations - his original use of mythology, his complex and concentrated **imagery**, his range through the whole spectrum of the English language." Indeed, as late as 1846, the influential De Quincey could write of the poet that "upon his mother tongue, upon this English language, has Keats trampled as with the hoofs of a buffalo." In 1845, all the copyrights of the poet's works and rights in his unpublished manuscripts were sold for only fifty pounds, a reprint of the poems in 1840 sold poorly, and in 1836 Keats' friends decided against putting up a monument to him in England because "his fame was not great enough to warrant it."

NEW INTEREST

But in the midst of all this neglect, a new generation was springing up to whom, as one critic has put it, Keats spoke with the authentic voice of poetry. Among the poet's youthful defenders was Richard Monckton Milnes who, taking over from Keats' friend Brown, published in 1848 his *Life, Letters and Literary Remains of John Keats*, a book which helped to establish Keats as one of the greatest artists of his generation. Some readers went even further in their praise. Often moved as much by the poet's pathetic but heroic life as by his books, they began ranking him among the very greatest writers of all time, even the eminently thoughtful and respectable critic Matthew Arnold saying of him, "He is with Shakespeare."

PRESENT - DAY CRITICISM

It would be impossible even to list here all of the critical and scholarly works that have been written about Keats in the twentieth century. (A few of these titles appear in the Bibliography.) His works have gone through many editions, dozens of volumes of criticism and biography have appeared, with such a major critic as T. S. Eliot confirming Arnold's judgment of the "Shakespearean quality of Keats' greatness," translations of his poems have appeared in some twenty languages, and he has survived, better than any of his contemporaries, the attacks on Romanticism in the early years of this century. The heroic nature of his struggle to create himself a poet in his own image, his technical mastery, the richness and integrity of his poetic structures, able to stand up under the most rigorous modern criticism, the warmth and humanity of his letters - all these matters and many more have been the subjects of books and articles. Nor does it seem likely that his poems will ever fall from the eminence they have achieved. There can be no doubt that the prophecy which Keats made in all seriousness as he began work on "Hyperion" has been fulfilled: "I think I shall be among the English Poets after my death."

ESSAY QUESTIONS AND ANSWERS

Question: Discuss the poetic forms in which Keats wrote.

Answer: Keats was a constant experimenter with poetic forms and used most of those he attempted with great success, always striving to find the right **stanza** or the right line length for the story he wished to tell or the idea he wanted to express. The first poem of Keats' that we have is written in Spenserian **stanza**. It is, however, merely an exercise. The first form with which the poet really worked seriously was the **sonnet**, the form in which his initial masterpiece - "On First Looking into Chapman's Homer" - was written and which would later evolve into the **stanza** forms of the great odes. For his early meditative pieces, such as "Sleep and Poetry," his epistles, and his long poem "Endymion," Keats use rhymed **couplets** of iambic pentameter, carefully avoiding, however, the so-called end - stopped or heroic couplets which had helped to make Alexander Pope anathema to the Romantics. Indeed, some critics feel that Keats went too far in avoiding end-stops, especially in "Endymion." In any case, it is significant that none of the poet's best work was composed in this form. For his long narrative poems, Keats experimented with a number of stanzas. "Isabella" is written in ottava rima, eight-line **stanzas** with the **rhyme** scheme abababcc, and the poem's failure is to a certain extent a function of its form. The material of the poem is grisly, the stanza tends to create humorous effects, and the result of the combination is unfortunate. The Spenserian **stanza** Keats chose for "The Eve of St. Agnes" is another matter. The nine-line form, the last line with its six beats, is exactly right for depicting the sensual and sentimental adventure of Madeline and Porphyro. Only Shelley, in his **elegy** for Keats, "Adonais," used the form with comparable skill in the nineteenth century. By this time, Keats had begun to chafe at the limitations of the **sonnet**. What he had to say, while suitable to the **sonnet**, could no longer be confined within fourteen lines, so he began to experiment, first with the **rhyme** scheme, as in "On the Sonnet," and then in the different **stanzas** of the odes, stanzas which are composed of various elements of the **sonnet**. Finally, in the unfinished Hyperion poems, Keats used the **blank verse** of Milton's **epics** and used it effectively.

Question: What is "negative capability?"

Answer: "Negative capability" is a term used by Keats to describe the ability to experience life without attempting to impose one's personality upon it. Many things stand between a man and reality: his moods, his preconceptions, his prejudices. But if a man has negative capability, he is able to penetrate such barriers in order to get to the heart of reality; he is able to yield himself utterly to the experience, to become, so to speak, the object he is contemplating. One of the keys, then, to the "thinginess" of Keats' best work, to its extraordinary tactile reality, is the poet's exercise of negative capability, a quality which he himself defined as the ability to be "in uncertainties, mysteries, doubts, without any irritable reaching after facts and reason."

Question: Who were some of the key figures in Keats' life?

Answer: (1) Charles Cowden Clarke, son of the headmaster at Keats' school, a friend of the poet who encouraged his early efforts. (2) Leigh Hunt, a poet and editor who took Keats on as his protege, was instrumental in publishing the early poems, and influenced Keats' early style, not always for the better. (3) Benjamin Bailey, who helped introduce Keats to philosophy, encouraged him to read Milton and Wordsworth, and who, injudiciously revealing some of the facts of Keats' early life to a critic, gave him ammunition to use against the poet. (4) Benjamin Robert Haydon, an artist who was instrumental in placing the Elgin Marbles in the British Museum and who introduced Keats to Greek art. (5) Charles Armitage Brown, a friend in whose house Keats lived, with whom the poet wrote his play Otho the Great, who disapproved of Keats' involvement with Fanny Brawne and who collected a good deal of material on the poet which later formed the basis of Monckton Milnes' 1848 edition of literary remains. (6) Tom Keats, the brother whom the poet nursed through his last illness. (7) George Keats, another brother who emigrated to America, giving the poet an opportunity to write many of the letters which have proven so useful to biographers and such a delight to readers. (8) Fanny Brawne, an intelligent and lively girl to whom Keats was engaged, whom he deeply loved and of whom, on occasion, he was also deeply jealous. (9) Richard Woodhouse, an assiduous and faithful collector of Keats material. (10) Joseph Severn, an artist friend of Keats' who accompanied the poet to Italy and attended him during his last illness.

BIBLIOGRAPHY AND GUIDE TO FURTHER RESEARCH

KEATS' WORKS

Briggs, Harold Edgar, ed., *The Complete Poetry and Selected Prose of John Keats* (New York: The Modern Library, 1951). This edition, available in paperback (T48), prints Keats' poems in the order in which they were written, and permits a reader to study the growth of the poet's art. Also included in this volume are a selection of Keats' letters and some of the most famous (or infamous) reviews of his works.

Garrod, H. W., ed., *The Poetical Works of John Keats* (London: Oxford University Press, 1956). This is the Oxford Standard Authors Edition of Keats' poems, revised from the previous editions edited by H. Buxton Forman. The poems are printed here in the order in which they were originally published during and after Keats' life. There are a few helpful notes.

Rollins, Hyder E., ed., *The Letters of John Keats*, 2 vols. (Cambridge, Mass., 1958). The complete letters. Keats wrote no formal literary criticism, as Coleridge and Shelley did, and so it is to his brilliant letters that students go to learn not only about the poet's life but also about his literary principles.

Trilling, Lionel, ed., *The Selected Letters of John Keats* (New York: Doubleday Anchor Books, 1956). A large selection, in paperback, of the poet's letters, with an introduction and notes.

KEATS' LIFE

Bate, W. J., *John Keats* (Cambridge, Mass., 1963). One of the best and most recent biographies of Keats. It concentrates on the poet's writings and on his relation to tradition.

Colvin, Sir Sidney, *John Keats: His Life and Poetry, His Friends, Critics, and After-Fame* (New York, 1920), A pioneering biography, in the "life and works" tradition, which, while factually out of date, is still valuable for its critical discussions.

Lowell, Amy, *John Keats*, 2 vols. (Boston and New York, 1925). Like Colvin's book, this is a little outdated as far as biographical fact is concerned, but is still valuable for its insights into the works.

Ward, Aileen, *John Keats: The Making of a Poet* (New York, 1963). An excellent recent biography, tracing, through the poet's life and works, the gradual development of an artistic consciousness.

WORKS BY AND ABOUT KEATS' FRIENDS

Dilke, Charles Wentworth, *The Papers of a Critic*, selected . . . by his grandson, Sir Charles Wentworth Dilke, Bart., 2 vols. (London, 1875).

Edgcumbe, Fred, ed., *Letters of Fanny Brawne to Fanny Keats* (New York, 1937). One of the most important pieces of Keats scholarship. When it first appeared it cast a new light on the nature of Fanny Brawne's character and on the relationship between her and the poet.

Hunt, Leigh, *Autobiography*, 3 vols. (London, 1850). Hunt was Keats' first influential literary friend and arranged for the publication of the young poet's initial volume of verse.

Rollins, Ryder Edward, ed., *The Keats Circle*, 2 vols. (Cambridge, Mass., 1948). A principal source book of material by and about the poet and his friends.

Sharp, William, *The Life and Letters of Joseph Severn* (London, 1892). Severn, the young artist who accompanied the dying Keats to Italy in the winter of 1820, was honored all his life for the service he rendered the poet during his last months of life. He is buried beside Keats in Rome.

CRITICISM OF "ENDYMION"

"The Cockney School of Poetry - No. IV," *Blackwood's Magazine*, August 1818. This "clever, contemptuous and unscrupulous" essay was written either by John Gibson Lockhart, or John Wilson, or both. It was only the first of many critical rejections under which Keats would have to labor for most of his life.

Croker, John Wilson, "Endymion: A Poetic Romance," *The Quarterly Review*, XXXVII (April, 1818). Another of the early attacks on Keats, opening with the extraordinary confession that the reviewer has not read the poem beyond the first book. This is the essay that Shelley particularly alludes to in "Adonais."

Reynolds, John Hamilton, "The Quarterly Review - Mr. Keats," *The Alfred, West of England Journal and General Advertiser* (6 October 1818). A rousing defense of Keats by a friend.

Jeffrey, Francis, "Review of Endymion and Lamia, etc.," *The Edinburgh Review*, LXVII (August, 1820). A very belated, favorable review of "Endymion" which appeared in the influential *Edinburgh Review*. At this point, Keats had only six months to live. An earlier appearance of this essay could not have saved the poet's life but might well have relieved some of his financial distress.

(The above items, listed chronologically, have been brought together by Harold Edgar Briggs in the Modern Library editions of Keats' poems, listed above under Keats' Works. This book also contains letters by Shelley, Woodhouse, John Scott, and Benjamin Bailey, and Keats' own letters No. 14 and 15 of October 9 and 27, 1818, on the same subject.)

Briggs, Harold Edgar, "Keats' Conscious and Unconscious Reactions to Criticism of Endymion," *Publications of the Modern Language Association*, LX (December, 1954), 1106 - 1129.

DISCUSSIONS OF PARTICULAR POEMS

Bate, Walter Jackson, "The Ode To Autumn" from *John Keats* (Cambridge, Mass., 1963).

Bloom, Harold, "The `Ode to Psyche' and the `Ode on Melancholy,'" from *The Visionary Company: A Reading of English Romantic Poetry* (New York, 1961).

Brooks, Cleanth, "Keats' Sylvan Historian: History without Footnotes," *The Well Wrought Urn* (New York, 1947). This is one of the most famous of literally hundreds of commentaries on the "Ode on a Grecian Urn."

James, D. G., "The Two Hyperions," from the *Romantic Comedy* (London, 1948).

Perkins, David, "`Lamia' and `The Ode to a Nightingale,'" from *The Quest for Permanence: The Symbolism of Wordsworth, Shelley, and Keats* (Cambridge, Mass., 1959).

Stillinger, Jack, "The Hoodwinking of Madeline: Scepticism in 'The Eve of St. Agnes,'" *Studies in Philology*, LVIII (1961).

Wasserman, Earl, "The 'Ode on a Grecian Urn,'" from *The Finer Tone: Keats' Major Poems* (Baltimore, 1953).

(Most of the above essays have been brought together by Walter Jackson Bate in the anthology entitled *Keats*, published in 1964 by Prentice-Hall as part of its Twentieth Century Views series. The book is in paperback.)

KEATS' ART

Bate, Walter Jackson, Negative Capability: The Intuitive Approach in Keats (Cambridge, Mass., 1939).

___, The Stylistic Development of Keats (New York, 1945).

Finney, C. L., The Evolution of Keats' *Poetry*, 2 vols. (Cambridge, Mass., 1936).

Fogle, R. H., "Empathic **Imagery** in Keats and Shelley," *Publications of the Modern Language Association*, LXI (1946), 163.

Ridley, M. R., Keats' *Craftsmanship* (New York, 1933).

Roberts, J. H., "Poetry of Sensation or of Thought," *Publications of the Modern Language Association*, XLV (1930), 1129.

Tate, Allen, "A Reading of Keats," *American Scholar*, (Winter 1945 - 46).

Wright, W. F., "A Sudden Development in Keats' Poetic Method," *State College of Washington Studies*, VIII (1940), 113.

www.ingramcontent.com/pod-product-compliance
Lightning Source LLC
LaVergne TN
LVHW011732060526
838200LV00051B/3150